Dancing in Montreal

Seeds of a Choreographic History

Iro Tembeck

Translated from the French and revised by the author

Studies in Dance History
The Journal of the Society of Dance History Scholars
Volume V   Number 2   Fall 1994

Memory is a form of courage
—Jean Vilar

Tis by our lack of ghosts
we're haunted
—Earle Birney, from the poem "CanLit"

Acknowledgments

This book is the first step in an attempt to map the choreographic terrain of Quebec during the past six decades. The documentation comes from many sources, including chance readings and encounters. Numerous people, both famous and lesser known, have contributed to the growth of dance in Montreal. Unfortunately, the need to limit this study to the choreographic and theatrical aspects of Quebec dance has made it impossible to acknowledge the role of all these pioneering dancers and teachers. They have unfailingly supported their art, given generously of their technical knowledge, and shared their love for dance with students and colleagues. Without their help and insights, neither the dances, the choreographers, nor the institutions that emerged would have developed the way they did or figured so prominently in this book. To all these craftspersons of the dance I extend my gratitude, trusting that their contributions will be given their full due in other studies.

Funding for this study of Quebec dance was provided by a research grant from the Social Science and Humanities Research Council of Canada (SSHRC). The publication of the original French version was made possible by a grant from the Canadian Federation of the Humanities, with additional help from the Publications Committee of the Université du Québec à Montréal (UQAM). This committee also contributed funds toward the publication of the present English version.

I would like to express my deep appreciation for the help and information provided by the following:

Miriam and Lawrence Adams, for allowing me to consult their Dance Collection Danse archives in Toronto;

Jill Officer, retired faculty member of the dance department of the University of Waterloo, Ontario, for making available documents from her research project, originally entitled *Dictionary of Canadian Dance*;

Rose-Marie Lèbe-Néron, of the Université de Montréal, for sharing with me the material in her possession on early Montreal dance;

Vincent Warren, a former premier danseur and now historian and librarian of Les Grands Ballets Canadiens, for giving me access to the dance library of La Maison de la Danse;

Jill Marvin, for reading the first draft of the English translation of this book;

Selma Odom, for rereading the translation and offering valuable comments;

René Fortin and Gilles Saint-Pierre, of the Audio-Visual Services of UQAM, for faithfully reproducing the original photographs included in the book;

Last but not least, Lynn Garafola, for her patient and thorough editing of the English version.

My sincerest thanks also go to the following dancemakers for their eyewitness accounts and oral histories, which helped to shape my view of dance in Quebec over the years: Miriam and Lawrence Adams, Suzanne Blier-Cantin, Jean Fournier de Belleval, Michel Boudot, Andréa Cadet-Roy, Ghitta Caiserman-Roth, Ludmilla Chiriaeff, Christina Coleman, Francis Coleman, Marie Côté, Gérald Crevier, France Desjarlais, Juliette Fischer, Peter Flinsch, Paul-André Fortier, Lise Gagnier, Eva von Gencsy, Margie Gillis, Françoise Graham, Martine Haug, Eric Hyrst, Vanda Intini-Perreault, Daniel Jackson, Irene Kon, Pierre Lacasse, Maurice Lacasse-Morenoff, Paul Lapointe, Pierre Lapointe, Ginette Laurin, Emily Lawrence, Aline Legris, Daniel Léveillé, Brian Macdonald, Alexander Macdougall, Phyllis Margolick, Jill Marvin, Andrée Millaire, Michael Montanaro, Eleanor Moore-Ashton, Birouté Nagys, Fernand Nault, Brydon Paige, Yvette Pauzé, Sheila Pearce- Lawrence, Jean-Pierre Perreault, Anne-Marie Peters, Linda Rabin, Jeanne Renaud, Françoise Riopelle, Roger Rochon, Randy Saharuni, Geneviève Salbaing, Elsie Salomons, Tom Scott, Ann Naran Silverstone, Daniel Soulières, Suzanne Stapells, Linda Stearns, Françoise Sullivan, and Vincent Warren.

I.T.

Contents

List of Illustrations

Introduction

Although dance has existed throughout the ages, it has not always received the attention it deserves, even among dance artists and enthusiasts. In Quebec and in English Canada generally, research in dance history is still in its infancy. Few in number, dance scholars face innumerable obstacles, not least of which is the scarcity or nonexistence of accessible sources.

To examine dance from an historical perspective demands an approach that enables us to define the place that dance occupies in a given society; this, in turn, will shed light on its role, functions, and meanings. An ethnographic approach to dance history extends the horizons of the art itself, broadening our knowledge of its social interactions, while allowing for a global vision of the social and cultural factors determining its development.

As Janet Adshead[1] and others have noted, historical perspectives allow the historian-observer to establish direct or indirect links between events, so as to analyze their relevance to the process of social charge. The study of history is a quest not only for facts but also for causes. When applied to dance, it enables us to trace its rise and continuing development as an art form, while also explaining the character of its evolution. Ignoring the cultural context leads to a superficial treatment of the facts and an equally superficial analysis of the history they map. By the same token, it is only by considering the social aspects of dance that we can see where art and politics intersect.

Charting the Territory

Because the history of Quebec dance is virtually unexplored, there is a natural temptation to deal with the subject in its entirety. To avoid this, it has been necessary to establish strict temporal, geographic, and aesthetic boundaries. This study examines the history of professional dance in Quebec, and specifically in Montreal, during the past six decades. As a cultural metropolis, Montreal was the site of virtually all of the province's creative activities in dance, to the point that the terms "Quebec dance" and "Montreal dance" are often used interchangeably in this book. This investigation spans several decades beginning with the Great Depression in an attempt to explain the origins of the explosion of dance activity in Montreal during the 1980s that led to national and international recognition. Because traditional folk dancing has been studied elsewhere, it has not been included.

Although it breaks new ground, this study of the history of dance in Quebec does not claim in any way to be definitive. It aims, rather, at whetting the reader's curiosity and stimulating much-needed research by revealing unknown or forgotten episodes of Quebec's dance past. Instead of delaying publication until the completion of a full study, I have chosen to share my work as it now stands, recognizing that my ideas may well be revised in light of future discoveries.

Methodology

When analyzing dance from a sociocultural perspective, we often proceed by way of edu-cated guesses based on retrieved fragments of documentation. Since the works them-selves are long gone, we rely on secondary sources to chart their passage through time. The task is all the more difficult because the field of Quebec dance is as yet unmapped: the researcher must explore it like a scout, open it up like a pioneer. The problem is not one of rereading or rethinking the subject, but delineating or "writing" it for the first time. In this archaeological adventure, the historian necessarily dons the cap of the histo-riographer.

The methodological framework of this study is inspired by the theories of two French historians: Michel Foucault and Henri-Irénée Marrou. Foucault's method, or "archaeo-logical" approach,[2] seeks to reconstruct and elucidate the past by studying not only its major but also its minor trends, its continuities as well as its ruptures, what has been done together with what has not been done: from the whole emerges a total vision of real-ity. Thus, along with more obvious trendsetters, lesser-known dance figures are discussed in this book, although without necessarily giving full-fledged accounts of their short-lived contributions: the primary aim has been to document their presence.

By contrast to Foucault, Marrou[3] regards the writing of history as a task akin to that of the creator-interpreter: the historian reconstructs the events from a personal viewpoint. He seeks to "interpret," and in so doing retrieves the often-forgotten aspect of "creation" and "creativity" inherent in his task. As a creator and recreator, he illuminates the shaded areas that awaken his interest, analyzing both recurring and "suspended" historical phe-nomena, as he perceives them. Viewed from this perspective, history is indeed open to a multitude of possible readings.

By its very nature, history is never static. Fluid and in constant flux, it demands con-stant requestionings; future revisions are thus not only inevitable, but also desirable. Indeed, several years will almost certainly elapse before an exhaustive inventory of Que-bec dance sees the light of day. Only after the necessary spadework has been done will it be possible to measure the true significance of dance's numerous contributions to Que-bec and Canadian culture.

A methodological caesura exists in this study between the treatment of dances created prior to 1965 and those of more recent vintage. The beginnings of professional dance in Quebec are analyzed from a "funnel" perspective. The chapters open with a description of the sociopolitical and economic landscape, then pass to a discussion of the cultural and artistic context, and, finally, to an analysis of the role of dance in the society of the peri-od. Since reconstructions do not exist, older dance works are viewed from a sociocultural perspective, without attempting to examine them critically. By contrast, recent works need less contextualization and lend themselves to greater critical appraisal because of the availability of film and video recordings.

Despite a growing interest in the cultural phenomena of societies past and present, dance remains a neglected field of research. The first stumbling block is the general view of dance as a frivolous activity undeserving of serious consideration. Another, as Debo-rah Jowitt reminds us, is that we always run the risk of seeing history through the eyes of the present.[4] We subscribe to the arrogant belief that today's craft far surpasses the achievements of the past. Rather than measuring the individual or collective contribution of each dance artist in terms of his contemporaries, we apply the criteria of present-day performers and technique. In order to reconstruct and understand the past, we must learn to detach it from the present.

Long ostracized by an ultra-conservative church and state, dance in Quebec has had to struggle to achieve respectability. Unfortunately, old attitudes still linger. Dance cannot hope to become a legitimate field of study until the public-at-large comes to perceive it as a form of high cultural endeavor. As Jean Trudel writes so eloquently:

> Dance matters. Linked by its very essence to the body, it is the basic tool, the master key opening the door to individual and social space. Dance presents itself as the final end of this conquest, that is, as cosmic mastery, transcending not only the individual and time, but also the arbitrary language of historicity to become collective, timeless consciousness.[5]

I
Quebec Society:
From the Turn of the Century to the Great Depression

*The roots of contemporary Quebec lie far in the past. We do not believe
that today's Quebec was suddenly born with the Quiet Revolution or
the Second World War: it is the product of a secular evolution.*[1]

Cultural Landscape and National Fabric

During the first third of this century, Catholicism retained a strong hold on Quebec.
Urbanization, underway since the 1850s, continued unabated. By the turn of the century, one-third of the Quebec population consisted of city dwellers, a percentage higher
than anywhere else in Canada. French Canadian society remained heavily influenced
by Catholic, Jansenist ideology, with a persistence of social values associated with a
traditional way of life.

Although the beginnings of industrialization dated to the mid-nineteenth century,
the change from a rural to an urban society occurred gradually. Indeed, historians such
as Paul-André Linteau believe that it was only in the 1930s, in the wake of the Depression and during the difficult interwar period, that Quebec reached its first significant
watershed on the long road to modernity.

A hundred years ago, the traditional character of Quebec society alienated it from
the progressive climate existing elsewhere in North America. Québécois* values were
stable and well-entrenched. The population as a whole had little interest in social
change. Extended families were typical, and the birth rate was higher in French Canada
than in the rest of the country. Overpopulated villages caused many to settle in urban
centers. By 1900, one-quarter of the French Canadian population was concentrated in
Montreal and its suburbs, making the city the economic center of Canada.

As a commercial metropolis, Montreal served as an important crossroads between
eastern and western Canada. The rural areas of Quebec were exploited by mining
industries, and its natural resources were an economic asset. Although limited in numbers, by the early 1900s the French Canadian bourgeoisie was beginning to make itself
felt as a political force, especially on the provincial level.

By contrast to the industrial bourgeoisie, which was largely English-speaking or
Anglophone, the Francophone presence was concentrated in the middle class. Some
French Canadians occupied key posts in banking institutions and chambers of com-

---

*The term "Québécois" has several meanings. It refers to French Canadians living in Quebec and to
French Canadian cultural values intent on preserving a French presence on an English-speaking continent.
It also refers to the ideology that seeks to bring about Quebec's separation from the rest of Canada. The
term "Quebecker," on the other hand, refers to all residents of the province who are either of English
descent or of non-French ethnic origins.

merce as well as in the business press and other specialized publications catering to groups such as manufacturers and shopkeepers. For the labor movement, the period prior to the 1920s was one of militancy and expansion. Class tensions grew more acute. Alarmed by the threat posed by industrialization, the Catholic clergy actively resisted all forms of change. However, its opposition came too late: with the growing strength of the labor movement, the process of modernization was already slipping from church control. In this era, too, Quebec welcomed its first wave of immigrants from southern and eastern Europe, the newcomers being mostly Italians and Polish Jews.

During this turbulent transitional period, two ideologies, two visions of society, confronted each other in Quebec. Liberalism, supported by the political class and the business community, favored economic growth, progress, and free enterprise—all regarded as essential to the development of society as a whole—in addition to advocating an improved educational system. Opposing this was the ideology of clerical ultra-nationalism, which took a pessimistic view of economic change and adopted a stance of protectionism and cultural isolationism. Shunning foreign influences, this ideology advocated a return to the forms of rural society and the preservation of Catholic values. Nevertheless, industrialization and modernization continued to gain ground.

For all the changes taking place, Quebec remained culturally backward. Brother Untel (better known as Jean-Paul Desbiens) summed up the contradiction succinctly: Quebec was "a country where one lives a time lag of two-and-a-half revolutions: clocking into America, but on medieval time."[2]

In 1927, the bishops expressed similar fears in a statement that underscored the strategic rejection of the present:

> A wind of sensualism blows from foreign lands over our beloved country. Ways of thinking and living, incompatible with Catholic principles, are corrupting Christian consciences and spreading with alarming speed.[3]

The growth of the nationalist movement in Quebec led to a questioning of Quebec's place in Canada's cultural fabric. In this several factors converged—the First World War, the Conscription Law of 1917, the ideological turmoil within the Québécois community itself—all of which served to intensify the alienation and isolation experienced by Quebec to an ever greater degree. Only in the 1930s would a revolt against tradition take place.

The Artistic Scene

This sociocultural and economic context, foregrounding the themes of religion and nationality, affected the growth of the arts in Quebec. Within the limited sphere occupied by dance, the struggle was all the more complex. Subordinate to cultural mores, dance had no place in the social fabric of Quebec, at least so long as society remained in the grip of the Catholic clergy. However, according to Gérard Morisset, the 1920s represented a significant moment in the evolution of Quebec artistic practice.[4] The Exposition des Arts Décoratifs, which opened in Paris in 1925, was an important source of inspiration and innovation for visual artists. Alfred Pellan, one of the first graduates of the Ecole des Beaux-Arts founded in Montreal in 1920, traveled to Paris to immerse himself in the new artistic ideas. At the same time, following the recommendation of the Commission on Historical Monuments, a law was passed for the preservation of Quebec's heritage. Meanwhile, CKAC broadcast the first French-language radio programs in North America. The Symphony Orchestra of Montreal was founded in 1934, a year after the establishment of a provincial museum. As for Quebec City's Symphony Orchestra, this had been in existence since 1906.

Evolution of Theater Practice

Theater developed more rapidly than dance in Quebec. Even if the clergy did not always look kindly on dramatic art, certain theatrical events were condoned, especially those associated with religious pageants. The first venue devoted exclusively to theater in Quebec was the Theatre Royal, also known as the Molson Theatre, which opened its doors to the English-speaking public as early as 1825. Three-quarters of a century later saw the creation of its French equivalent, the Théâtre National, situated where the Metropolis discotheque now stands.[5] Professional Francophone theater was heavily influenced by Anglo-American theater and owed its initial survival to Anglophone support. In fact, Francophone theater practice was caught between the French classical tradition, on the one hand, which ultimately bored the Quebec audience, and, on the other, Broadway-style vaudeville, which appealed to it. At the same time, a new type of melodrama proliferated. This consisted of religious dramas and mystery plays where Christian piety merged with Christian fervor in passionate dramatizations of the life of Christ. *La Passion*, created in 1902 by Germain Beaulieu, was one such play. Eventually banned by the archdiocese, the production attracted 35,000 spectators during three weeks of performances.[6] For the average Québécois, religious drama satisfied the need for a more popular culture. *Aurore l'Enfant Martyre* (1920), which became the prototype of Québécois melodrama, enjoyed success after success for several decades.

Café-concerts were also popular in this period, as were vaudeville and variety shows. In 1909, *Ohé Ohé Françoise* became the symbol par excellence of the musical revue with Québécois content.

Modernist euphoria characterized the theatrical climate of the Roaring Twenties. American mass culture was the model, and silent films were very popular. An entertainment industry linked to consumer culture became widespread.

Other noteworthy events of Montreal theatrical life were Sarah Bernhardt's appearances in 1880, 1888, and 1917. Her first visit caused a scandal, because of a play the clergy deemed immoral. However, her popularity and the cult that surrounded her added a political dimension to her stage presence. Her stay in Montreal prompted an artistic awakening among French Canadians thirsty for artistic freedom.

The English section of the Montreal Repertory Theatre was founded in 1930, although its French counterpart would only appear several years later. Pierre Gauvreau, a Francophone artist of many talents, participated in MRT productions. After a brief stint as a dancer with Gérald Crevier, Gauvreau made his mark as an Automatist painter before winning fame as an actor and playwright. Finally, there were the *Soirées de famille*, "family evenings" that offered instruction in speech and deportment, along with exercises, probably of Delsartean origin, to enhance physical well-being.

The creation of institutions beyond the influence of the clergy sowed the first seeds of a new lay culture. An important step had been taken in closing the gap between Quebec and the rest of North America in matters of learning and culture.

The Clergy and Dance: From the Pulpit to the Flesh

A physical activity par excellence, dance has always borne the wrath of the Church in Quebec. Indeed, until as late as 1950, the social practice of dance was limited to three forms of expression:

- traditional folk dances that were part of everyday life in New France and were typically performed at evening gatherings during the harsh Canadian winter;
- balls and dances that were part of the leisure activities of both the grand and petty bourgeoisie and offered an ideal way of forming social relationships within a pleasant, genteel setting;
- musical revues that were frequently incorporated into artistic entertainments for the cultured elite.

For whatever reason, these three kinds of activity escaped vilification by the clergy from the pulpit. However, the French Canadian temperament considered dancing a necessity. Undoubtedly, this had something to do with the Latin origins of the populace, as well as the need for amusement during long winter evenings. At such *veillées*, as they were called, families gathered around the hearth to sing, tell stories, play the fiddle, and, as the crowning activity of the evening, to dance. According to Jean Trudel, the traditional dances of these *veillées* were both the catalyst and the common denominator of an effort to transcend existing institutions.[7] Indeed, dancing incited French Canadians to brave the punishments of the clergy. Love of dance was so deeply ingrained in French Canadians of the eighteenth century that Sieur Pierre de Sales Laterrière the Elder was moved to state: "Never have I known a people that loved dancing more than 'les Canadiens.'"[8] ("Canadiens" was the name that the inhabitants of New France had given themselves long before the term was understood to refer to the whole country of Canada.)

It is obvious, however, that dancing was an activity mainly practiced by the English-speaking population, which was chiefly non-Catholic and thus not subject to Catholic interdictions. A French Canadian popular song of the eighteenth century suggests how dance was viewed in traditional Quebec society, while also revealing the influence of the clergy over its flock:

> Let us cast aside the regrets of the lass who was damned
> For loving too well dances and receptions,
> Let us listen to her sobs, the cries of her pain,
> Let us, touched by her misfortune, be more reserved.[9]

Similarly, many Québécois folk tales depict the devil as a handsome dancer leading the faithful astray. The best-known of these tales is that of Rose LaTulippe, a maiden who is seduced by the devil-turned-dancer and dies.

Pastoral Letters, Tracts, and Clerical Admonitions

During the early colonial period, the dwellers of New France endured the restrictions of the Church both on their social pastimes and on theatrical performances. According to the edict published in 1700 by Monseigneur de Saint-Vallier, the following dangers were to be avoided:

> With regard to Comedies, Balls, Dances, Masquerades, and other dangerous spectacles, we renew our edict of 16 January 1694, exhorting the beloved members of our diocese to be aware that all such care as we have given to their salvation shall prove useless, should they become party to the devil's pomps and works.[10]

Toward the middle of the eighteenth century, Abbé Gosselin exhorted his faithful to flee the example of high society, with its balls and other profane entertainments.[11] By 1843, however, Monseigneur Bourget had qualified somewhat the prohibition on dance:

> Dances, unless organized to evil end by placing others or oneself in danger of yielding to the temptations of the flesh or to any other peril, are not bad in themselves and represent not the pleasures of the flesh, but simple merrymaking. If one wishes young people to abstain from illicit pleasures, one must allow them others that are honest. Here are the rules that I would suggest to attain so important a goal. I found them in St. Antonin, as cited by St. Ligouri in the aforesaid book and treatise: dances are permitted, so long as they are conducted by laymen, for honest people, and in decent fashion.[12]

Despite his relatively open attitude toward balls, Monseigneur Bourget voiced certain reservations:

> 1. That there be no work, nor song, nor gesture, nor dance, nor games contrary to modesty;
> 2. That parents themselves accompany their children, without ever allowing their daughters to be alone with young men of their acquaintance;
> 3. That these gatherings do not extend long into the night.
> 4. That no alcohol be served except in the course of a family repast that may accompany such gatherings.[13]

The apogee of clerical power, so to speak, was reached in Quebec toward the end of the last century. That the public view of artists was strongly influenced by the attitude of the church is made clear from an article by J.P. Tardivel published on 27 December 1880 in *Mélanges*:

> Actors and actresses [and, by extension, dancers] are public entertainers. In society, they occupy the same position as the bear trainer, the clown, the circus equestrian, the zoo keeper, and the puppeteer, and have no more right to an ovation.[14]

Finally, Monseigneur Bruchési evoked the harmful and corrupting effects of the theater on the faithful:

> In the same way, [men of the theater] are apologists for all dishonest intrigues and the worst disorders. They call to their aid licentious scenes, those *féeries*

and those ballets where the lightness of the dresses, the sensuality of the poses, and the voluptuousness of the evolutions constitute a veritable attack on public modesty.[15]

One could also add to these examples a last admonition by Abbé Victorin Germain:

> If a young man or a young girl, in their secret private lives, are in the habit of a solitary sin that they wish to correct, one cannot deny that many relapses are indirectly caused by the practice of sensual dances, which awaken evil memories, dormant instincts, and calmed senses, troubling the will and causing them in short order to succumb once more to weakness, defeat, and despondency.[16]

In other words, dance was perceived as an invitation to onanism! This text becomes all the more significant when we discover its source: a book entitled *Dansera-t-on chez moi? un cas de conscience* (A Case of Conscience: Are We to Dance at Home?).

An Archaeological Portrait of Dance in Montreal

The clergy's negative attitude was an important factor in keeping the organization and practice of dance to a minimum. No local professional troupe seems to have existed, despite the appearance both in Montreal and Quebec City of dance studios catering to amateurs. Popular dances and balls constituted practically the only form of dance activity, and can thus be considered the antecedents of local theatrical and art dance.

The earliest patrons of theatrical dance in Montreal were mainly well-to-do families of English origin. Such families would almost certainly have been aware of the work of Steele MacKaye, the Delsarte disciple who paid repeated visits to the city between 1881 and 1914. Montreal was also fortunate in being the first North American port of call for many international dance and ballet companies. An engagement at theaters such as His (or Her) Majesty's, the Gayety (today's Théâtre du Nouveau Monde/Comédie Canadienne), and the Théâtre Saint-Denis was often the first stop on the North American touring circuit. Moreover, as a bicultural center, Montreal held a special fascination for foreign artists. Although British theater stars were chiefly esteemed by the English-speaking community, dance artists, having no language barrier, could theoretically appeal to the elites of both French and English origin, although, in practice, this was seldom the case.

Thus, Montreal's higher-income families discovered the innovative theater of Loie Fuller and her sister Ida in 1909, and savored the charm of Toronto-born Maud Allan in 1916. In 1914, Ruth St. Denis appeared, while the legendary Anna Pavlova came in 1909 and again in 1922. As for German expressionist dance, there was Mary Wigman, who performed in Montreal during her 1930-1931 North American tour, followed, not long after, by Harald Kreutzberg and Yvonne Georgi. In the classical field, there was the Mordkin Ballet, which appeared in 1927. Three years later, La Argentina proved that there was a market for Spanish dance as well. In 1927, Charles Weidman, a renegade from Denishawn, stopped in Montreal, while in 1924 and 1929, the Isadorables—Anna, Lisa, and Margot Duncan—danced in Quebec's cultural capital.

On the local scene, the discoveries were fewer. The oldest Montreal ballet studio that can be documented dates to the eighteenth century: here, Louis Renault taught classical dancing from 1737 to 1749.[17] The dancing master Dulongpré had a school from 1787 to 1790, while Antoine Rod offered dancing classes from 1799 to 1820. Another teacher, Joe Belair, also opened a studio in this period.[18] Miss S. Aspinall, a student of the renowned Auguste Vestris, is believed to have taught in Quebec City from 1820 to 1836, while the English-born dancer Anne Hill opened a school in Montreal in 1843.[19] Finally, a New Yorker by the name of W.J. Lewis opened a dance academy in Montreal in 1863.

Frank Norman

In 1890, *Dancing*, the first periodical dedicated exclusively to dance, noted that among the members of the newly formed National Association of Teachers of Dancing of the United States and Canada was a certain Frank Norman of Montreal. Norman taught dancing, deportment, and folk dancing at Montreal's Stanley Hall. An advertisement published in 1900 in *La Presse*, the city's French-language daily, announced the school's selling points: "Classes in dance and good posture. Bilingual. Easy method. No failures. Private classes."[20] Another announcement, published five years later, boasted that the academy "had the city's largest and most exclusive French Canadian clientele."[21] Norman wrote a technical manual on social dancing and was the sole Canadian representative to the International Congress of Dance Masters held in Vienna in 1911. A well-informed man, he kept abreast of developments in dance teaching throughout the world. In 1914, he boasted of having attracted 35,000 students of all ages to his academy.

Ezzak Ruvenoff

Another notable dance teacher in Montreal was Ezzak Ruvenoff, a former soloist of the Imperial Ballet in St. Petersburg.[22] Despite such impressive credentials, his life is poorly documented. He was born in 1874 in the Ukrainian city of Kiev. At the age of sixteen he became the first Jewish dancer to attain the rank of soloist, Alexander II having temporarily lifted the ban against admitting Jews to the Imperial Ballet.

During the Russian Revolution, Ruvenoff was arrested for his loyalty to the Tsar and immediately condemned to forced labor in a Siberian camp. He escaped two years later, borrowing a boat that foundered in the turbulent waters off Russia's Far East coast. Eventually, he was rescued by a Japanese fishing boat. In the course of this ordeal, Ruvenoff temporarily lost the power of speech, and the Japanese, believing him to be Canadian, dropped him off in Vancouver. From Vancouver he made his way to Montreal, where he arrived in 1922.

Montrealers who knew Ruvenoff well describe him as an aristocrat *manqué*, a man of luxurious tastes. He opened two ballet schools, one at the corner of St. Catherine Street in downtown Montreal, and the other on St. Lawrence Boulevard. Here, he taught ballet according to the method advocated by Friedrich Albert Zorn, a German who had worked in Odessa. Zorn's method stressed good muscular coordination and difficult adagio exercises to build endurance. Ruvenoff, however, seldom gave combinations that traveled across the floor, and his exercises at the barre were said to be very strenuous. Among his best-known students were Gérald Crevier, Gina Vaubois, Elsie Salomons, Phyllis Salomons Margolick, Eleanor Moore-Ashton, and the sisters

Dorothy and Verna Evans—all of whose names appear in the souvenir programs for Ruvenoff's annual recitals. These young dancers would form the next generation of ballet masters and dance teachers in Quebec. The most illustrious among them was Crevier, who would become a key figure in the Montreal world of classical dance.

Ruvenoff posed a real threat to other Montreal teachers of the period, who could not compete with his professionalism and knowledge of classical dancing. Although a strict disciplinarian, he brought to his teaching a passion for dance. Emulating Enrico Cecchetti, he used a cane in class, prodding students as he corrected their placement and physical alignment. At that time, it was a common practice for teachers to rent ballrooms in downtown hotels for their classes. Ruvenoff recruited a good part of his clientele by teaching at the Sheraton Mount Royal, located in the very heart of the city.

Fortune smiled upon him when the Allen family from Toronto opened twenty-three theaters across Canada. These theaters formed the nucleus of the Famous Players group, and Ruvenoff was engaged as producer. During these happy years, his combined annual salary from producing and teaching was said to be $250,000, an extraordinary sum for the time. As a producer, he often traveled to the United States and to the United Kingdom. He lived like a millionaire and basked in the admiration of his Montreal students.

In 1939, a tragic accident brought his career as a ballet master to a sudden end. During one of his recitals at Montreal's Imperial Theatre, the costume of a young pupil caught fire. Two little girls were burned alive in the panic, and several others were disfigured. His reputation broken, Ruvenoff sank into a deep depression and spent two years at the Royal Victoria Hospital before being released.

In 1949, at the age of seventy-five, Ruvenoff returned to teaching. However, despite support from Montreal's Jewish community, he gradually dropped from sight. The once famous artist, credited by many as bringing Russian classicism to Canada in the 1920s, passed away in 1970 alone, impoverished, and forgotten.

George Shefler

George Shefler was another teacher who opened a dance studio in Montreal in the 1930s. His school offered a wide range of classes in social dance, ballet, show dancing, and tap. Shefler also organized a summer camp where youngsters could study dance in addition to taking part in sports. The annual performances of the Shefler Springtime Revue were very popular among parents and guaranteed the school a steady clientele. Micheline Pétolas, a prize pupil who took the stage name of Micheline Lane, went to New York, where she danced at the Radio City Music Hall beginning in 1934. She also studied at the School of American Ballet directed by George Balanchine.

Dance in Higher Education

In the field of dance education, McGill University, Canada's oldest institution of higher learning, was surprisingly progressive. Indeed, credit-bearing courses in creative and interpretative dance were offered as early as 1929, only three years after the first American universities officially established dance degrees. Organized under the auspices of the physical education department, McGill's courses were open to men as well as women. Anglophone Montreal was thus well aware of the artistic experiments underway in American institutions. Among McGill's first graduates was Elsie Salomons, who later became a pioneer in creative dance. She worked for many years to include this in the curriculum of the city's English educational system.

Another McGill graduate was Nina Caiserman, whose sister Ghitta Caiserman-Roth was an important Montreal painter. Nina left for New York in the 1940s and danced with Martha Graham, later joining the New Dance Group. In the 1940s and 1950s, she also danced for Anna Sokolow and took part in the famous summer programs at the Connecticut College School of Dance. Noted for her expressiveness, she went on to teach at Sarah Lawrence College and at the New Dance Group. She also gave a solo concert on Broadway where she appeared in her own choreography. Her career, alas, was cut short by suicide.

From these retrieved fragments of the past one gleans the first stirrings of professional dance in Quebec. The story, little known even now, testifies to the appearance of an art that was alternately ignored, misunderstood, and anathematized, an art, however, that also endured, without losing the essence of what made it unique.

II
Classical Ballet, French Canadian Style

Montreal: From the 1930s to the End of World War II

By the late 1930s, Quebec was plunged in misery.[1] Religious fervor mounted among the faithful, who sought a palliative from economic woes. The crisis brought a momentary halt to urbanization. Unemployment and poverty became widespread, with the working class being the most affected. The onset of the Second World War further aggravated the divisions within Quebec society. On one side stood a communist-oriented left-wing movement; on the other, a nationalist revival fueled by anticommunism, xenophobia, and even anti-Semitism.

Maurice Duplessis, the head of the Union Nationale party, became prime minister of Quebec in 1936. The role of the state expanded, especially with regard to the economy. The Padlock Law, passed in 1937, called for the immediate closing of any enterprise suspected of promoting communist ideology. Sworn to the preservation of Christian morality, both church and school kept a heavy grip on the lives of most French Canadians. At the same time, censorship assured the church a say in all cultural institutions. Save for the years 1939-1944, when the Provincial Liberal Party was in power, the Duplessis regime governed Quebec for nearly twenty-five years, until 1959.

A key feature of the Quebec public school system in this era was its religious character. Two separate boards governed the system: the Catholic School Commission, for pupils of Catholic faith, and its Protestant counterpart, for students of other denominations, who were enrolled in separate schools. Universities and *collèges classiques* were chiefly attended by children of the cultural and economic elite. The absence of any kind of coordination among the programs of these various institutions compartmentalized the system, which had a detrimental influence on the standard of French Canadian education and general culture. Most French Canadian men worked in factories. Their female counterparts, even if more active than before, continued to perform traditional roles as wives, mothers, and homemakers.

The Cultural and Artistic Realm

Heavily influenced by the United States, a new cultural model came to the fore in Montreal in the 1930s and 1940s—mass entertainment. After 1930, vaudeville-style stage shows were often presented with films on a combined program. Many dancers found work in the prologues that supplied the "live" entertainment for such programs, which attracted large crowds to the theater. Meanwhile, the arts catered to an educated and financially comfortable public. For Francophone society, however, practically the only cultural centers that existed were seminaries. Yet despite the severe censorship of the Duplessis years, when a long list of books were placed on the Index and, thus, off-limits to pious Catholic readers, a profound desire for freedom was gradually and quietly stirring.

Slowly, the arts made progress. The year 1933 saw the opening of Quebec's provincial museum; three years later, the Canadian Broadcasting Corporation (CBC) radio network was established. The following year, French radio-plays and melodramas in the style of *Aurore l'Enfant Martyre*, and the radio broadcasts of Gratien Gélinas brought a more popular tone to artmaking, while nourishing the interest of the average Québécois in theatrical performance. In 1937, too, thanks to the unflagging devotion of Father Emile Legault, Les Compagnons de Saint-Laurent was founded, bringing a breath of fresh air to Quebec's French-language theater. A year later, the Union des Artistes, the first performing arts union, was formed, along with the National Film Board. In the early 1940s, the Conservatoire d'Art Dramatique et de Musique was founded, and a French section was added to the Montreal Repertory Theatre. Finally, in 1945, Hugh MacLennan published his celebrated *Two Solitudes*, a novel that spoke to the city's divided cultural identity.

Maurice Lacasse-Morenoff

Until his death in 1993, Maurice Lacasse-Morenoff was Montreal's oldest living dance pioneer, a veritable monument of its choreographic past. Born in 1906, he took his first social dance classes at the age of six in the studio of his father Adélard Lacasse, who was himself the son of Antîme Lacasse, an outstanding fiddler in the French Canadian tradition. Adélard (whose real name was Abondius) had studied to become a notary, but changed careers when hardships befell the family and financial reversals caused his parents to lose their farm.

Forced to leave his country home, Adélard found himself in need of a job. He became a schoolteacher in Montreal and organized *Soirées de famille*—or community family evenings—where he also taught social dancing. In 1894 or thereabouts, a group of friends and would-be patrons raised the money to send him to New York. There he took Oscar Dureya's course in "modern" dances, which ranged from the minuet to the waltz, and even included the cakewalk. Adélard later returned to New York for refresher courses, this time studying with Irene and Vernon Castle.

In 1895, Adélard opened a dance studio on St. Lawrence Boulevard. He attracted numerous students eager to learn the fashionable dances of the time. His son Maurice, soaking up this atmosphere from earliest childhood, showed a natural talent for dancing. Maurice soon became his father's assistant; he demonstrated the dance figures to the other students and in time ended up teaching the combinations himself.

In 1925, lightning struck: Maurice fell in love with a student, a Frenchwoman of Spanish origin named Carmen Sierra (1905-1990), with whom he eloped. For the next fifty years Carmen would be his partner in art and in life, as well as his muse. She also became his assistant ballet mistress, in addition to making the costumes for their recitals and other theatrical ventures.

Their careers took off thanks to a lucky break. In 1925, the Capitol Theatre in Montreal had engaged a company of Russian balalaika musicians and dancers. When one of the dancers became injured, the tour manager, John Appleby, asked Maurice to take over and present one of his own acts. Maurice and Carmen became overnight celebri-

Maurice and Carmen Morenoff in *Danse Apache*, North American tour
(1926-1931). Photograph by Celebrity Studio, Chicago. Morenoff Archives, UQAM.

ties, developing a style based on the toe, tap, and acrobatic routines so popular at the
time.

Theatrical Agencies soon booked them for a North American tour that lasted for
five years, from 1926 to 1931. Crisscrossing the continent, the couple played the best
vaudeville houses, music halls, and night clubs in North America. Dancers of the period, even artists as illustrious as Pavlova, did not scorn engagements on the variety
stage. The more traditional theaters, reserved mainly for music concerts and opera, seldom opened their doors to performances made up exclusively of dancing. Nor were
there any venues that catered solely to dance.

During this lucrative North American tour, Carmen and Maurice joined forces with
the American tap dancer Bill Albright. Together, they created an act that they baptized

Maurice and Carmen Morenoff in an acrobatic adagio, North American tour (1926-1931). Photograph by Celebrity Studio, Chicago. Morenoff Archives, UQAM.

the Parisian Trio. Around this time, Lacasse adopted a Russian-sounding name, as did many dancers of the period in the wake of Diaghilev's Ballets Russes: it was a good marketing and publicity strategy. The name of Morenoff was probably borrowed from Sergei Marinoff, who had a school in Chicago and taught ballet by correspondence: Carmen had given Maurice a copy of his technical manual as a gift. From then on, the pair would be known as the Morenoffs. (Another theory is that the name was an acronym, a combination of *MOR*-ice and carm-*EN*, with the *OFF* ending to make it sound Russian.)

  Returning to Quebec, the Morenoffs appeared on the Montreal night club circuit, while continuing to teach at the Lacasse studio, now relocated on the outskirts of the city. Around 1933, Morenoff took over the studio from his father, who died in 1936. To the existing ballroom, tap, character, and acrobatic dance classes, Morenoff added classes in classical ballet. The studio thrived, only closing its doors in 1986, by which time it had been in existence for ninety-one years, a feat all the more remarkable in that it occurred in Catholic-dominated Quebec.

Morenoff's knowledge of ballet was self-taught. He familiarized himself with the aesthetic canons of classicism by poring over books and technical manuals, an approach that was not only idiosyncratic, but also highly unusual. On his curriculum vitae, instead of listing the teachers with whom he had studied, he listed the titles of works in his personal dance library, along with the date of their purchase, and a précis of his various readings. As a teacher, his method was largely based on Sergei Marinoff's system, which he had studied by correspondence. Oddly enough, given his eagerness for new knowledge, it apparently never crossed Morenoff's mind to see what was happening in other Montreal studios.

Morenoff's teaching style was as eccentric as his study methods. Newcomers were obliged to take private lessons and to memorize a series of exercises for each lesson. They then joined a group class for those exercises they had already mastered, after which they returned to private classes to memorize other combinations. Only after a student had fully mastered the set exercises of the Morenoff "method" would he or she be admitted to a group class on a regular basis. In addition, Morenoff would distribute exercise sheets to his students illustrating the combinations they had just learned: these sheets, intended as a study aid, were the weekly homework. This personalized method of learning was not new to the studio. Adélard Lacasse had already written his own ballroom dance manual, *La danse apprise chez soi* ("Dancing Learned at Home").

For all the idiosyncracies of his teaching method, Morenoff attracted many French Canadians to his school. Indeed, the Morenoff studio became the breeding ground for the first generation of male dancers who would pursue international careers. It was at the Morenoff studio that Fernand Nault, Roland Lorrain, Marc Beaudet, and Michel Boudot first learned to dance. Nault left Quebec to join American Ballet Theatre, where he remained for twenty-one years as a character dancer and ballet master, before returning to Montreal to assume the post of assistant director of Les Grands Ballets Canadiens. Lorrain became a soloist with the Marquis de Cuevas company, Ballet International, while Beaudet joined the New York City Ballet. Boudot, for his part, danced with Ruth Sorel in Quebec, then with London Festival Ballet, and finally with Les Grands Ballets Canadiens.

This proliferation of male dancers marked an important milestone in the development of Quebec dance. Despite the clergy's negative attitude toward dance, and especially toward young men who chose it as a profession, Morenoff's own relationship with the clergy was amicable. Wooed by the church, he staged several religious pageants, including one, in 1952, at the request of Cardinal Léger. By then, Morenoff's reputation had traveled beyond the province. As early as 1945 he was invited to mount a pageant in Winnipeg with 200 participants to commemorate the one-hundredth anniversary of the founding of the community of Oblate fathers in Manitoba.

Meanwhile, in the microuniverse of his studio, Morenoff, assisted by his wife, prepared his annual recitals. The first recital took place in 1935; the last, more than fifty years later, in 1986. Beginning in 1945 these annual events were called Le Ballet Music Hall Morenoff. The repertory included court and character dances, Spanish numbers, and jazz routines with such carefree titles as *East Side Story*. (The east end of Montreal was French Canadian.) Morenoff also created frankly theatrical pieces like

ABOVE: Le Ballet Music Hall Morenoff in *Tango Apassionato*.
Morenoff Archives, UQAM.

LEFT: Maurice and Carmen Morenoff posing outdoors in the Laurentian Mountains.
Pierre Lapointe Archives, UQAM.

Bolero Apassionato, which, to judge from the photographs, revealed a modernity that easily rivals certain contemporary dance-theater works.

Morenoff's unquenchable thirst for knowledge about the many facets of dance prompted him to read widely. To share this knowledge of the dance past with his students, he covered the walls of his studio with photographs and documents organized by theme or period and illustrating different types of dancing. For students waiting in line to perform their enchaînements, such displays had much the same impact as the lecture-demonstrations that helped create a knowledgeable public for dance in the United States.

The Morenoff studio was located in a triplex in the east end of Montreal. The walls of the ground floor apartment had been torn down to increase the space for dancing. The building was very *fin de siècle*, with stained glass windows, wood paneling, and embossed plaster work. The atmosphere was both old and new, lending a sense of timelessness to the work at hand. Such time-traveling was also typical of Morenoff's annual recitals, where tableaux vivants evoking civilizations past often shared the bill with very contemporary works. In keeping with this eclecticism, publicity for the school stressed that it offered "the most complete and best informed [instruction] in all types of dancing."[2] In the Morenoffs' desire to create a "university of the dance," their enterprise revealed an affinity with Denishawn. But this was not the only similarity between the two. Like Ruth St. Denis and Ted Shawn, the Morenoffs were a professional couple. Their work had a strong theatrical bent, and even if they never became as famous as their American colleagues, they performed the same role with respect to Canadian dance as the Denishawn couple played in American dance: both were founding parents.

As performers, the Morenoffs made their mark chiefly as acrobatic adagio dancers. For this reason, they were perceived by their Montreal contemporaries as eccentric dancers rather than artistic purists. Nevertheless, it was to Morenoff that the dances for Les Variétés Lyriques were entrusted from 1936, when the theater was founded, to 1955, when it finally closed its doors. *Rose-Marie*, a musical comedy with a Canadian theme, was among the high points of Morenoff's career with Les Variétés Lyriques, which modeled its shows after the Théâtre du Châtelet in Paris. International stars, such as Luis Mariano, Rudy Hirigoyen, and Tino Rossi, appeared as guest artists in these productions, which brought a whiff of theatricality and show business to Montreal. As meticulous as he was dynamic, Morenoff kept notebooks in which he wrote down not only the choreography but also the production details for each show, including the lighting design, stage direction, and even at times the musical arrangement. He did the same thing for his own recitals.

Morenoff's personal dance library was a collector's dream. Never having crossed the ocean, he kept abreast of developments overseas through books. A complete autodidact, he had learned from books to give free rein to his imagination when choreographing. His dramatic flair, his innate musicality, and his deep respect for the art of dance gave a professional touch to his endeavors at a time when professionalism was at low ebb in his hometown. But it was his love of dance that he best conveyed to his dancers and students. For all their differences of opinion, critics agreed that he "knew how to make good use of the strengths and limitations of his interpreters."[3] And despite limited financial resources, his performances were always accompanied by live music.

Maurice Lacasse-Morenoff was the only French Canadian dance pioneer of his generation to receive press coverage in *Dance Magazine* and *The Dancing Times*. But he was also a loner, who seldom participated in group events, a rare exception being the Canadian Ballet Festival held in Montreal in 1951. This partly explains why his contribution has been relegated to the shadows. Moreover, with the disappearance of Les Variétés Lyriques in 1955, his work became less visible, especially as he was never invited to choreograph for the new television variety shows that supplanted other forms of popular entertainment. Theatrical, eclectic, and idiosyncratic, Morenoff was a forerunner of the dance-theater so representative of Montreal choreography today. His work, spanning a half-century, was the harbinger of a modernity to come.

Gérald Crevier

Born in Longueuil in 1912 of an Irish mother and a French Canadian father, Gérald Crevier fell in love with dance after seeing the legendary Pavlova perform at Montreal's Orpheum Theatre in 1922. Shortly thereafter, he enrolled in Ezzak Ruvenoff's school, where he studied ballet according to the Zorn method. Crevier also took classes in tap with Dora Marshall, who had formerly danced at the Radio City Music Hall and now taught stage dancing in Montreal.

His first professional job, which Dora Marshall obtained for him, was dancing in the musical interludes on movie programs. She also trained him to be a dance captain for vaudeville shows, and it was on one of these shows that he met Elisabeth (Zette)

Gérald Crevier teaching Lise Gagnier at his studio.
Lise Gagnier Collection.

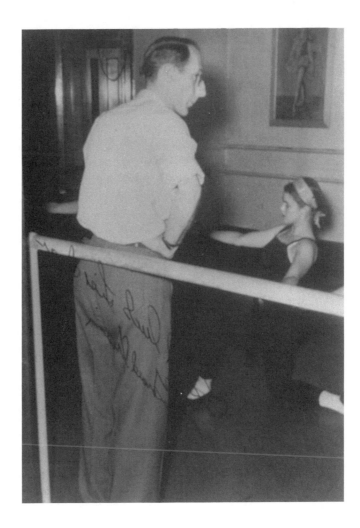

At the barre in Gérald Crevier's studio. From left: Jeanne Daoust, Lise
Gagnier, Pierrette Imbleau, Aline Legris, Jacqueline Boisvert, Andrée
Millaire, and an unidentified pupil. Aline Legris Collection.

Devaux, a dancer from the French West Indies, whom he eventually married.

It was Zette who persuaded Crevier to go to England in 1932. During his two-year
stay in London, he joined the corps de ballet of the Sadler's Wells company (the forerunner of today's Royal Ballet), directed by Ninette de Valois. To make money, he
danced at the Piccadilly Hotel supper club, and at the same time taught show dancing
and tap, Hollywood musical comedies being immensely popular in Europe during the
1930s.

On his return to Montreal in 1934, he was offered a job at the Shefler school, but
decided, instead, to open his own school. Classes were held in the Berkeley Hotel ballroom, which he rented. Many of Shefler's students followed him, including Andrée
Millaire. Other students came from Montreal's French schools: among them were Lise
Gagnier, Aline Legris, and Françoise Sullivan, then at the start of her career as a ballerina. Like his colleagues, Crevier organized annual recitals, which he produced under
the name of "Dansart."

When the Second World War broke out, Crevier enlisted, serving with the Canadian
army in England. During his leaves, he took classes with Phyllis Bedells, an early pioneer of the Royal Academy of Dancing (RAD) method. This teaching system appealed
to Crevier because of its methodical approach and the set examinations that monitored
the student's progress. Back home, he became the first Montreal teacher to adopt the
RAD system and to hold the required examinations, with examiners brought in from
the United Kingdom. Crevier's academy had an excellent reputation and was consid-

Françoise Sullivan in costume for a Dansart recital. Françoise Sullivan Collection.

ered the best Montreal studio for classical training.

Lise Gagnier was the first Québécoise to pass the RAD advanced professional examination. RAD technique was taught regularly in Montreal until the 1970s, when its popularity waned. In addition to his pioneering work as a teacher, Crevier founded Les Ballets-Québec, the province's first chartered ballet company. Formed in 1948 (although it was only chartered in 1949), the troupe had an unusually large roster of dancers for the time—thirteen women and nine men. Françoise Sullivan, Lise Gagnier, James Ronaldson, and Jacques Delisle were some of the soloists. The company performed throughout the province, as well as in Montreal. The repertory was classically-based and included excerpts from nineteenth-century ballets, such as the *Swan Lake*

Les Ballets-Québec: Lise Gagnier and James Ronaldson in Gérald Crevier's
Veillée d'armes. Lise Gagnier Collection.

pas de deux. *Veillée d'armes* (1950), based on a scenario by Alex Pereima, one of the company's dancers, was among Crevier's most successful works as a choreographer. In 1950, he choreographed the Walpurgis Night scene in the opera *Faust*, which was presented under the auspices of the Montreal Summer Festival and featured dancers from his company. They also appeared at the outdoor festivals held at Montreal's Chalet Mont Royal. In 1951, moreover, Les Ballets-Québec was among the companies singled out at the Third Canadian Ballet Festival, another Montreal event.

Although it was Quebec's first professional dance company, Les Ballets-Québec was not destined to survive. Shortly after the creation of the National Ballet of Canada, Celia Franca, who directed the Toronto-based company, offered lucrative contracts to six of Crevier's dancers. Deeply discouraged by their loss to the rival enterprise, he decided to close shop. With this, his dance career came to a sudden end. He retired to a farm in Ontario, and after several years moved to Venice, Florida. Suzanne Blier-Cantin, former president of Les Ballets-Québec, took over his dance studio, where she continued for some years to teach the RAD method. Crevier eventually returned to Ontario, where he died in 1993.

With the passing of Morenoff and Crevier, Montreal lost its oldest links with the city's dance past. Almost exact contemporaries, the two represented the first generation of Montreal dance pioneers, even if their paths seldom crossed. But they knew of each other's work, and through the legacy of their students, they remain a presence even today.

III
Newcomers from Europe

The Aftermath of the Second World War

During the postwar period French Canadians suffered a triple handicap. Not only did they lag behind the Anglophone population culturally, they also did so in business, while the reactionary Duplessis government limited their access to information.[1] Practicing Catholics continued to look to the parish for guidance. Both church and state favored a return to nationalism and posed as defenders of the established order. Nevertheless, a process of secularization was underway, and this jostled traditions. A new Francophone elite began to voice its opposition to the ideology of the clergy and the politics of the regime, sowing the seeds of what would later be referred to as the "Quiet Revolution."

The strike of asbestos workers in 1949 marked a political turning point. Calls for modernization and for an end to the Duplessis government began to be heard. Pierre E. Trudeau and Gérard Pelletier founded *Cité Libre*, a neoliberal journal that attacked Quebec's historical and cultural backwardness. On the federal level, the Royal Commission on National Development in the Arts, Letters, and Sciences (1949–1951), better known as the Massey-Levesque Commission, revealed the fragility of Canadian cultural organizations—lack of funding, heavy American influence, an ideology of materialism. Not unexpectedly, the music hall retained its popularity.

In painting, the Group of Seven continued to hold sway, as it had since the 1920s. Although the artists of this group espoused a new approach to art, their aesthetic values were far from radical. Their pictures were pleasant and harmonious, in the tradition of "beautiful" painting, while their treatment of Canadian subject matter reflected a vision of cultural uniformity that shied from depicting national differences.

In 1948, the group of rebel artists around the painter Paul-Emile Borduas took the courageous step of signing the famous manifesto *Le Refus Global*. In putting their names to this statement of "total refusal," they signed the death warrant of reactionary, provincial Quebec, while raising the banner of individual freedom. They demanded that Quebec society become more secular and cast off its cultural blinders. *Cité Libre* had promoted a similar internationally-minded vision. Whether in religion or politics, the signatories demanded cultural pluralism.

At the same time that this radical, new movement emerged within the Francophone elite, an exciting period was opening in English Canada. The war had left it yearning for new cultural horizons. With the passage of an immigration law that gave artists the same favored status as skilled workers, a wave of foreign artists entered the country. Most came from eastern and central Europe, and were fleeing Nazi persecution and totalitarianism. Some remained only briefly in their new country, before returning home. Others used Canada as a stepping stone to New York. Still others decided to stay, and would make an important place for themselves in the Canadian cultural fabric.

This wave of artist/immigrants brightened the cultural landscape throughout Canada. Many artists elected to settle in Quebec, and among them were the writers, philosophers, painters, set designers, and dancers who made their home in Montreal. They brought with them impressive credentials and an intimate knowledge of new artistic practices and techniques. Immigrating to Canada was a symbolic gesture: they came to the New World to find a freedom of expression that no longer existed in Europe. Abandoning Europe for a new land, they had chosen, so they thought, the path of freedom and affirmation. An irony of fate awaited them: if Quebec was virgin territory for the artist, it also offered him no means of support.

Ruth Sorel

Ruth Sorel, née Abramowitz, is a striking example of the refugee artists who came to Quebec after the Second World War in flight from Nazi horrors and anti-Semitism. Born in 1907 in Halle, Germany, to Polish parents, she had studied the Dalcroze method and been a student of Mary Wigman in Dresden, dancing for this celebrated artist from 1923 to 1928. She also pursued a parallel career as a character dance soloist at the Berlin Opera, where she worked from 1927 to 1933 under the direction of Bruno Walter. During this period, she won critical acclaim for her interpretation of Potiphar's Wife in *Legend of Joseph,* choreographed by Lizzy Maudrick in 1930.

Ruth Sorel.
Studio portrait by Steele, Toronto.

Cover of Les Ballets Ruth Sorel souvenir program, 1949.
Pierre Lapointe Archives, UQAM.

Sorel left Germany in 1933, settling in Poland with her stage partner George Groke. From 1933 to 1935, they made several continental and overseas tours, appearing in Italy, France, England, and Palestine, as well as Canada and Brazil. They not only choreographed their own dances, but also starred in them. Among their better-known works was the Dance of the Seven Veils from *Salomé*, a theme that had inspired numerous artists since the turn of the century. Other items on their program were *Pair of Lovers at Evening's Rest*, *Joan of Arc*, and *Death Lament*, all of which revealed a strong sense of theatricality. A dancer of compelling stage presence, Sorel took the first prize in performance at the International Dance Competition held in Warsaw in 1933, despite steep competition. She was later described as "having the feet of Pavlova and the hands of [Uday] Shankar."[2]

Returning to Warsaw after her world tour, Sorel opened a school for professional dancers and actors. She also taught young people. Chartered by the Polish Ministry of Education, the school came to international notice in 1939 at the dance competition that took place that year in Brussels, where her students won prizes and special mentions. During her extended stay in Poland, she married Michel Choromanski, a Polish playwright and man of letters. Together, they emigrated to Montreal in 1944.

Once in Montreal, Ruth gave a solo concert that was well received by Montrealers. Shortly after, she opened a dance studio at the Westmount YMCA and formed a small group, which was billed alternately as Les Ballets Ruth Sorel and the Ruth Sorel Modern Dance Group. Although her choreography belonged to the tradition of German expressionist dance, her works were eclectic in style. Some, like *Suite en blanc*, were classically inspired; others, like *Biographie Dansée*, were dramatic monologues. Sorel also mounted psychological ballets, such as *Tittle Tattle (Papotages)*, and even experimented with medieval styles, as in *Mea Culpa Mea Culpa*. Some of her pieces, including *Two Lawyers in the Moonlight*, revealed humorous touches. Although she often turned to world literature for inspiration, as in *Shakespearean Shadows*, she sometimes asked her husband for scenarios. One of these was for her 1949 *La Gaspésienne*, subtitled *Vie d'une mère canadienne*, the first ballet with a Canadian theme, and a Québécois one at that. Reviewing the work, the French-language daily *Le Droit* noted that "thanks to the constant efforts of certain choreographers and company directors, the Canadian public is witnessing the birth of an authentically Canadian form of ballet. *La Gaspésienne* is a striking example of this."[3]

Les Ballets Ruth Sorel represented Quebec at the First Canadian Ballet Festival, organized by David Yeddeau and Gweneth Lloyd in Winnipeg in 1948. That same year the company also danced in New York at the Choreographers' Workshop, a rare event for a Quebec dance ensemble. Members of her company included Andrée Millaire, the first Québécoise ballerina to enjoy an international career; Alexander Macdougall, a former dancer with the Jooss Ballet; Birouté Nagys, a dancer from Central Europe, and, finally, Michel Boudot.

In the mid-1950s, Choromanski and Sorel left Canada and returned to Warsaw, where Sorel died in 1974. The reason for their abrupt departure is unknown, although it may have had something to do with the lack of financial support for artists in Canada. Another possibility is that political pressures compelled their presence in Poland. Even today, an aura of mystery lingers over their memory.

Elizabeth Leese

Born in 1916 of mixed Danish and German descent, Elizabeth Leese spent her childhood in Germany. Her father, a disciple of Teilhard de Chardin, was a professor of philosophy at Hamburg University. Leese began her modern dance studies in Germany, and later trained in classical ballet with Lubov Egorova, the former Maryinsky ballerina who had opened a studio in Paris in the 1920s. Leese then went to Switzerland, where she joined Trudi Schoop's modern dance company, which toured North America in 1937, when Leese visited Canada for the first time. An injury brought her dancing career to a temporary end. Convalescing in England, she attended classes at the Jooss-Leeder School, studying theatrical and dramatic techniques with a view to applying them to dance.

In England she met the Canadian journalist Kenneth Johnstone, whom she eventual-

Portrait of Elizabeth Leese. Irene Kon Collection.

ly married. This enabled her to enter Canada, despite her German passport. Anti-Ger-
man feeling ran high in Canada during the interwar years, and anti-Semitism was also
widespread. The couple settled in Toronto in 1939. Leese was relieved to be in Canada,
even though her family was still in Germany. She was quickly engaged by the Volkoff
Canadian Ballet, the biggest dance company in Canada, directed by Boris Volkoff. A
character dance soloist, she appeared in modern and so-called "plastique" works. She
also gave classes in pantomime and modern dance at Volkoff's school. After three
years in Toronto, she moved to Ottawa, where her husband joined the staff of the
National Film Board.

The Canadian capital was a cultural desert during the war years. Leese became a
city employee, setting up a full-scale recreational dance program. She taught classes in
modern, ballroom, tap, and folk dancing at the city's Recreational Association. She
also produced musical revues for soldiers on leave, building a solid reputation for herself. She made frequent visits to New York during this period, keeping up with the lat-
est developments in modern dance.

In 1944, the couple moved again, this time to Montreal, where Leese immediately
opened a school and formed a company. Those who worked with her describe her as a
striking Nordic beauty, with a personality as compelling in real life as onstage; they
also speak of her generosity as an artist. Although she was chiefly a modern dancer by
training and experience, as the years passed, she found herself increasingly drawn to
ballet.

Before arriving in Canada, she had mastered the modern dance techniques associated with German expressionism. In Montreal, she extended her knowledge of modern
dance by taking summer courses in the United States with Martha Graham, Doris
Humphrey, and Hanya Holm, while studying ballet with Antony Tudor, Margaret
Craske, Edward Caton, and George Balanchine. Despite the growing appeal of ballet,

Leese herself was not only too tall to be a sylph, but also too overtly expressive.

Her Montreal school was the first to offer a teacher training program. Leese believed that training teachers was as important as training dancers. She introduced the Cecchetti method to Quebec, enlisting the help of respected teachers such as Margaret Saul. Aside from her pioneering work in classical dance teaching, she also taught a form of modern dance that blended American and German styles. The school thrived from 1945 to 1960. Among the students who became famous were Brian Macdonald, Jeanne Renaud, Juliette Fischer, Jacqueline Lemieux- Lopez, Yves Cousineau, Alexander Macdougall, and Birouté Nagys.

Elizabeth Leese teaching at her Westmount studio. Irene Kon Collection.

As a choreographer, Leese favored the purity of line associated with ballet, and the emotionalism and expressive qualities characteristic of modern dance. Her most celebrated work was *Lady from the Sea*, after the play by Henrik Ibsen, which had an original score by Saul Honigman and sets designed by Jean Fournier de Belleval. The piece was first danced by Leese's company in 1952. Subsequently televised, it met with such success that it was produced by the National Ballet of Canada in 1955, with Celia Franca dancing the title role originally created by Leese. In the interim, however, the choreography was revised to make it more classical. Unlike the original version, the National Ballet production was danced on pointe.

Leese's professional career extended beyond the school and its recitals. Intelligent and cultivated, she advocated a cosmopolitan approach to the arts, even in Montreal, where she worked with a variety of artistic and cultural organizations. She was active in theater as well as dance. With the same ease that she had moved from modern dance to ballet, she now shuttled between the city's French and English theater worlds. She performed the title roles in *I Remember Mama* and *Anna Christie*, which were produced by the Montreal Repertory Theatre, and arranged the choreography for Jean Anouilh's *Bal des voleurs*, staged by Les Compagnons de Saint-Laurent. She was also a commentator on French radio and worked with Gratien Gélinas on the premiere of *Ti-Coq*.

In 1956, her student Brian Macdonald asked her to join his newly formed Montreal Theatre Ballet, a collective of local choreographers and dancers. Its aim was to promote Canadian talent in the fields of music and design, as well as in choreography and dancing. For all its good intentions, the company lasted no more than two years. In 1958, it folded for lack of funds.

Leese's versatility as an artist was also reflected in her participation in the *Revue Bleu et Or* at the Université de Montréal, and in its English counterpart, the *Red and White Revue*, at McGill University. Nor was she content merely to work in live theater. She choreographed dances for television that were broadcast on shows such as *Chants et danses du monde*, *Café des artistes*, *Montréal Panorama*, and *Carrefour*.

By 1960, when her school was showing signs of decline and her health was beginning to fail, she developed close ties with Les Grands Ballets Canadiens. Two years later, she died of a brain tumor. She bequeathed her personal library to Les Grands Ballets Canadiens, which created a scholarship in her name to help talented students continue their training.

Séda Zaré

A story of mysteries and promises, hopes and shattered dreams: this was Séda Zaré's life in Canada.

She was born in 1911 in the oil-producing city of Baku, in what is today Azerbaijan. Her parents were Armenian and, thanks to her father's tankers, well-off. In 1921, the Turkish massacre of Armenians forced the Nercessians to flee to England, where Séda was sent to boarding school. In England, she took her first dance classes, studying eurhythmics at the Dalcroze Institute and ballet with the celebrated Russian pedagogue Nicolas Legat. Séda's sister, Lia de Sirouyan, also studied eurhythmics, becoming an accomplished teacher and later working in Argentina. In addition, Séda took classes in "free" dancing with Margaret Morris and J. Gordon Denning.

She left England to study with Boris Kniaseff in Paris, eventually dancing in some

Séda Zaré during her dancing days in Berlin.
Photograph by Siegfried Enkelmann, Berlin. Séda Zaré Archives, UQAM.

of his productions. In the 1930s, she settled in Germany, where she lived from 1938 to 1950. During this period, she trained in Berlin at the classical studio of Alexandra Nikolaeva, who regarded her as a disciple and entrusted the studio to her when she retired.

Thus, Séda became the director of the Nikolaeva studio. By then, she had already obtained a certificate in choreography and a teaching license from the Deutsch Tanzbuhne—necessary professional credentials in Germany of the 1930s. One day, a young girl came to the studio; she was a beginning dance student, with a double-barrel name: Ludmilla Otzup-Gorny. Their paths would cross again after the war in Quebec: by then, the little girl had grown up and become the dancer Ludmilla Chiriaeff.

A classical dancer, Nercessian found herself in a country where modern dance, or "expressive" dance, as it was typically called in Germany, was in full swing. She became good friends with Rosalia Chladek, an important Ausdruckstanz figure, and took classes with her; she also studied with Harald Kreutzberg. She became, in turn, a soloist with the Berlin Opera, the Grosses Schauspielhaus, the Metropolis Theater, and the Deutsche Tanzbuhne. Forced to change her name, which sounded too ethnic to Nazi ears, she opted for the equally exotic—and Armenian—name of Zaré. During the war, she moved to Heidelberg, where she taught dance under the auspices of the German Youth Organization, while also organizing a number of performances. After the war ended, as Séda Zaré, she toured the capital cities of Switzerland, Holland, Norway, Denmark, Czechoslovakia, and Italy, under the sponsorship of the West German government. Typically, these were solo concerts, although dancers such as Robert Mayer, Karl Bergeest, Ivan Pinkusoff, and Ellys Gregor sometimes participated in the program either as soloists or as her partner in duets. The clippings in her personal scrapbooks are unanimous in praising her strong technique, expressiveness, flexibility, and the dynamic quality of her jump. Her versatility was such that once, when she needed money, she even spent a season touring with a circus. Needless to say, hers was the only classical act.

After the war, one of her brothers, who had already emigrated to Canada, was sent to Germany with the Canadian armed forces. Her persuaded his sister and her husband, Souren Saharuni, an Armenian journalist and art dealer, to emigrate to Canada. In 1950, the couple, with their infant son Randy, entered Canada as political refugees. Soon after their arrival, however, her husband left her, and Zaré had to shoulder alone responsibility for the child's upbringing. The psychological and material burdens entailed by the separation would influence the course of her Canadian career.

Now the family breadwinner, Zaré set to work quietly, without fanfare, despite her previous accomplishments and the hardships she had endured in her previous countries of adoption. To make ends meet, she danced in nightclubs. Nevertheless, during her first year in Montreal, the sisters of Villa Maria asked her to stage the dance part of a pageant entitled *Le Jeu de la voyagère* honoring the order's founder, Marguerite Bourgeois. Zaré also taught in Montreal and took over Ruth Sorel's schools in the neighboring cities of Trois Rivières and Shawinigan, where she organized annual recitals for hundreds of students. Eventually, she opened a studio in Westmount that she named the Montreal Professional Dance Center. The city's dancers flocked to her Russian-style ballet classes. Gradually, she developed her own technique, which she called "Anatomie pratique." The most innovative aspect of the system was a complete floor barre, an idea she had picked up from Boris Kniaseff, but now modified and refined. Several students from the school went on to professional careers. Some, like Bernadette Beliveau, joined the National Ballet of Canada. Marie Côté danced with the Opéra de Lille. Judith Marcuse not only performed but also choreographed for Ballet Rambert.

The professionals who gravitated to Zaré's studio sometimes also danced for her. Milenka Niederlova, Tom Scott, Michel Conte, Jacqueline Lemieux-Lopez, Pierre Lapointe, Lise Gagnier, Irène Apiné, and Jury Gottschalks, took part in her productions of the 1950s and 1960s, as did her former pupils Bernadette Beliveau and Marie Côté when they were in Montreal. Zaré formed a company, Concert Ballet Group, in 1961, not long after the demise of the Montreal Theatre Ballet, in which she had also participated. Concert Ballet Group performed in Montreal and the surrounding region on several occasions in the next few years.

When she arrived in Canada, Zaré had been full of hope and ideas for professional projects. However, unlike certain European cities, Montreal in the 1950s had no institutional framework to promote the development of dance. The public, for its part, was

Séda Zaré teaching at her Westmount studio.

as ignorant of the recreational aspects of dance as of its professional side. As Zaré conceived it, her task was twofold. On the one hand, she had to define dance as a recreational activity; on the other, to promote it as a professional one through the creation of an institute or conservatory. As it turned out, her contribution would be in the field of recreational rather than professional dance, although she had all the qualifications to succeed in this field as well, save perhaps the most important—political savvy.

Throughout her years in Montreal, Zaré wrote numerous reports, memoranda, and proposals advocating the establishment of a professional dance academy in Quebec. She was consulted by the Parent Commission, which was planning a complete overhaul of education in the province. She addressed open letters to the Canada Council and numerous other official organizations, but none of her professional training projects was accepted. She had no choice but to use her professional expertise in the service of dance as a recreational activity.

Thus, the performances of Concert Ballet Group were produced in collaboration with the Parks and Recreation Service of the City of Montreal. Under the same sponsorship, she organized a dance festival in Lafontaine Park, and as early as 1953, she created summer ballet courses in Sainte-Adèle and Saint-Sauveur with the help of Agnès Lefort, an art connoisseur. In these outdoor and rural settings, she hoped to find an environment conducive to the study not only of ballet but also creative dance. Ever active, she was for many years the ballet representative to the Fédération des loisirs-danse du Québec as well as a highly respected member of the Quebec Dance Teachers Association. She exerted her greatest influence through these organizations.

As a choreographer, Zaré created a number of works that were performed by local professionals. She herself rarely appeared onstage: her career as a dancer was already behind her when she arrived in Canada. However, she did appear in a few televised broadcasts while collaborating as a choreographer with Les Compagnons de Saint-Laurent, and with the Théâtre de la Ruche, which mounted seasonal operettas. She also participated in the ethnic festivals of Montreal's Russian and Armenian communities.

In 1964, she was invited by the Dance Research and Study Center of Buenos Aires to give an intensive summer course at the Teatro Colón and the Teatro de la Plaza. Among other things, she taught her method of "Anatomie pratique" and Dalcroze eurhythmics.

Zaré's decision to open a studio in the affluent Westmount district was not an act of snobbery. Like many Montreal teachers before her, she chose the locale in order to circumvent a city law taxing establishments that offered private or group classes. As an autonomous borough within Montreal, Westmount was not subject to this law, which explains the proliferation of dance studios in the district beginning in the 1930s.

Zaré died of cancer in San Diego in 1980 while returning to Canada after a brief stay in Mexico. Her chief contribution was as a teacher and as a promoter of dance *outside* Montreal, in the larger province of Quebec. Had her personality been different, the repercussions of her work would almost certainly have been greater. Ever the nomad, she was also a loner working in isolation on the margins of Montreal dance-making.

IV

Classical Ballet on the Threshold of Legitimacy

The 1950s

The year 1952 marked a turning point in the history of dance in Quebec. For one thing, television arrived in Montreal. The event played a significant role in Quebec's social revolution, broadening the frame of popular cultural reference and fomenting a network of communication that ended the isolation of rural communities. Also in 1952, the Canadian Broadcasting Corporation (CBC) invited Ludmilla Chiriaeff, an immigrant artist newly arrived in Canada, to choreograph for the network's weekly variety shows. Thus, Les Ballets Chiriaeff was born. Finally, in that year, Cardinal Léger partially lifted the ban against dancing: now, for the first time, folk dance activities were permitted.

The artistic and cultural renewal of the 1950s was at least partly attributable to the artists and intellectuals who had signed the *Refus Global* manifesto. Nevertheless, most of these opponents of the Duplessis regime would soon go into exile. In search of a world open to new ideas and propitious to creativity, they went to New York or Paris. In fact, during their long years away from home, many received the kind of public recognition denied them in Quebec.

With such rebels temporarily out of the picture, artists in Quebec now pursued a more traditional course. With its mass appeal, television was the perfect vehicle for this. Just as the invention of photography had prompted a redefinition of the fine arts in the early twentieth century, so the advent of television prompted changes in the entertainment industry. Vaudeville and musical comedy attendance fell, and Les Variétés Lyriques was forced to close down. With the weakening of clerical power, new venues for intellectual and artistic exchange appeared. And television became an important employer, providing work for many actors, dancers, and musicians.

The inauguration of Montreal television more or less coincided with the publication in 1951 of the Massey-Levesque Commission's report on the state of the arts, letters, and sciences in Canada. The commission's recommendations called for a significant expansion of the cultural realm. This led in 1957 to the creation of the Canada Council, a government organization to subsidize the arts. The Council's initial charter made no mention of dance, an omission that suggests the low regard in which dance—the poor relation among the arts—was held. Nevertheless, the road to social legitimacy had been opened: cultural and artistic identity was henceforth something to be encouraged.

Meanwhile, in 1951, the National Ballet of Canada was founded by Celia Franca in Toronto. Its existence crowned previous efforts to heighten national public awareness of dance, such as the choreographic showcases organized under the aegis of the Canadian Ballet Festivals inaugurated in Winnipeg in 1948. In the early 1950s, however, choreographic growth came to a temporary standstill in Quebec. Gérald Crevier's Les Ballets-Québec disbanded when several of the dancers joined the National Ballet of

Canada. Les Variétés Lyriques also disappeared, unable to compete with the small screen.

A more positive note was the proliferation of cultural institutions independent of the clergy. The Conservatoire d'Art Dramatique opened in Montreal in 1954 and in Quebec City in 1958. The Comédie Canadienne replaced the Gayety Theatre, and the Théâtre des Quat'sous opened its doors. In 1956, the Université de Montréal's School of Music came into being.

The 1950s turned out to be a critical decade. The foundation for an artistic support system was laid, and progress was made in secularizing the culture at large. However, despite the partial lifting of the church's ban on dancing, the situation remained far from ideal. The following statement, issued by Cardinal Léger in 1952, reveals how much ground remained to be covered before dance could make a respected place for itself in Québécois society:

1. It is strictly forbidden to dance in any place within church walls.

2. Modern dances shall not be authorized in any place under church jurisdiction [parish halls, schools, colleges, convents, hospitals].

3. Folk dance evenings are permitted so long as the program is approved by the recreation committee [of which a priest was always a member].[1]

Les Ballets Chiriaeff

Although folk dancing had finally been accepted in Catholic life, ballet and creative dance were still regarded as occasions for sin. It is surely no accident that Germany and the United States, the two cradles of modern dance, were largely Protestant countries. The Protestant ethic had no quarrel with the idea of *mens sana in corpore sano*.

Although attitudes on the part of the Catholic clergy were beginning to change, it was television that gave dance its first real boost. In fact, throughout the 1950s, the small screen was the chief vehicle in promoting dance and introducing it to a new audience, while acquainting that audience with the dancer's and choreographer's craft. At the same time, CBC contracts gave a semblance of job security to many dancers living on the edge of poverty. Television work also cemented ties within the professional dance community. The main rallying point, so to speak, was the dancer, choreographer, and ballet mistress Ludmilla Chiriaeff. This charismatic and determined woman was soon perceived as the godmother of professional ballet in Montreal.

Born in the Latvian capital of Riga to a Russian father and a Polish mother, Ludmilla Otzup-Gorny began her dance studies at Alexandra Nikolaeva's studio in Berlin under the direction of Séda Zaré. Fleeing Hitler's Germany and its concentration camps, the young dancer went to Switzerland, where she worked at the opera houses in Lausanne and Geneva, and performed the leading role in a Swiss film, *Danse solitaire*. With help from the Fonds de Réparation des Réfugiés, she and her husband, the designer Alexis Chiriaeff, emigrated to Quebec in 1952.

Arriving at Windsor Station in downtown Montreal, she walked up to nearby St. Catherine Street. There, to her great astonishment, she saw her name on a movie marquee: *Danse solitaire* was playing at the theater. Interpreting this as a good omen, she was convinced that fate had brought her to Montreal. Her Canadian career was launched soon after her arrival when she landed her first CBC contract.

Les Ballets Chiriaeff: Sheila Pearce-Lawrence (left), Ludmilla Chiriaeff, and Eva von Gencsy in Eric Hyrst's *Drawn Blinds*, CBC/Radio Canada. Sheila Pearce-Lawrence Collection.

Founded in 1952 as a pick-up company, Les Ballets Chiriaeff was recruited from dancers living in Montreal and Ottawa. Young and enthusiastic, they learned their craft on the job. For all the company's television success, its first "live" performance only took place in 1955, when it appeared at the Chalet Mont Royal as part of the Montreal Summer Festival. Two seasons later, Chiriaeff created her version of Igor Stravinsky's *Les Noces*, again for the Montreal Summer Festival. The work was so successful that Mayor Jean Drapeau encouraged her to form an official company. Les Grands Ballets Canadiens was incorporated in 1958, although for years the presumption of its name continued to raise eyebrows. The company began operations with a modest $6,000 subsidy to cover its first season.

Les Grands Ballets Canadiens

The history of Les Grands Ballets Canadiens is riddled with oddities. To begin with, the company got started late: a full twenty years separate its birth from that of the Winnipeg Ballet Club in 1938 (the Club later became the Royal Winnipeg Ballet). Quebec's distinctive sociocultural history, especially the strong opposition to dance by the clergy, also retarded the development of professional dance in the province, not only in relation to the rest of Canada, but also compared to the United States. Meanwhile, the appeal of television caused many Canadian dancers to flock to Montreal.

Indirectly, Les Ballets Chiriaeff had been formed to meet the needs of television.

Les Grands Ballets Canadiens: Andrée Millaire in *Pas de Quatre*.

However, these close ties with television did not extend to the company's successor. The future of Les Grands Ballets Canadiens lay with the stage, not the screen. The repertory remained eclectic, however. Les Ballets Chiriaeff had drawn as much on neo-classical forms as on character dance, the commedia dell'arte, and romantic styles, a combination that distinguishes LGBC seasons even today. Never purist, the company-has even produced the occasional classic, such as *Giselle* and *Coppélia*.

Other choreographers shared the limelight with Chiriaeff in the 1950s. One was Eric Hyrst, an Englishman who had been a soloist with the Sadler's Wells Ballet, the New York City Ballet, and other important companies. Initially, he had danced with the Royal Winnipeg Ballet. However, the promise of greater job security offered by television brought him to Montreal, where he settled with his Winnipeg partner, a ballerina of Hungarian origin named Eva von Gencsy. Von Gencsy and Hyrst made frequent appearances as soloists with Les Ballets Chiriaeff. In addition, Hyrst created several classical and romantic-style works for the company. His involvement strengthened the classical side of the repertory; it would do the same for LGBC.

The new company grew steadily. In the second season, it was invited to dance at Jacob's Pillow, the summer dance theater directed by Ted Shawn in Lee, Massachusetts. Most of the works created in this early period were by Hyrst or Chiriaeff herself. Where Chiriaeff's choreography revealed a penchant for character dance, her strong point as a dancer, and appealed to a broad public, Hyrst's tended more toward romanticism. Only in 1965 would a new figure emerge among the choreographers in residence. This was Fernand Nault, whom Chiriaeff had convinced to return home.

The Nault Era

French Canadian by birth, Fernand Nault made his reputation in the United States. He received his early training in Montreal at the Lacasse-Morenoff school, which he attended for six years, and made his stage debut at Les Variétés Lyriques in shows choreographed by Morenoff. A lucky break took him abroad. When Todd Bolender was injured during (American) Ballet Theatre's visit to Montreal in 1944, auditions were held for a replacement. Nault was chosen. Signed for the remainder of the tour, he remained with ABT for twenty-one years. During that time, he became one of the company's leading character dancers and, thanks to his exceptional memory, a respected ballet master.

In 1965, at the invitation of Chiriaeff, Nault joined LGBC as coartistic director and resident choreographer, posts he would occupy for more than a decade. Chiriaeff her-

Les Grands Ballets Canadiens: Daniel Martin (left), Jacques St. Cyr (as the Swan), and John Shields in Fernand Nault's *Carmina Burana*. Photograph by Andrew Oxenham.

self now became deeply involved in professional dance training. In 1966, the Ecole Supérieure de Danse du Québec was founded, and as Quebec's first school devoted wholly to professional training, immediately subsidized. This was followed in 1975 by a pilot project for a dance concentration within the performing arts program at the Ecole Pierre Laporte, and in 1979 by the creation of a ballet concentration at the Vieux Montréal CEGEP (CEGEP stands for Collège d'enseignement général et professionnel and is the equivalent of a junior college). Chiriaeff was closely involved with all these undertakings.

The Nault era marked a transition for LGBC. Known locally and nationally, it now acquired an international reputation. During his first year with the company, Nault remounted two works that he had recently staged in the United States—*The Nutcracker*, which soon became an event on the city's cultural calendar, and *Carmina Burana*. Presented during Expo 67, *Carmina Burana* was a resounding success and made it possible for the company to undertake its first European tour the following year.

The 1969-1970 season was another milestone in the company's history. Two outstanding works were created that year by Nault. One was *Tommy*, a rock opera to music by The Who, which became the symbol of hippies and the flower power generation. *Tommy* was a box-office blockbuster with a track record of hundreds of performances. The work appealed to a new teenage audience that had no interest in ballet fairy tales but easily identified with the psychedelic world Nault had depicted. Although *Tommy* succeeded in popularizing classical ballet, the work could hardly claim to break new choreographic ground.

Les Grands Ballets Canadiens in Fernand Nault's *Symphony of Psalms* at St. Joseph's Oratory. Photograph by Andrew Oxenham.

The need to attract a substantially larger audience prompted the creation in 1970 of a small affiliated company, Les Compagnons de la Danse, a name that recalled Father Emile Legault's theater group, Les Compagnons de Saint-Laurent. In existence for three years, the new company was subsidized by Local Initiatives Projects (LIP) grants, a federal program aimed at reducing unemployment. The grants offered young and apprentice dancers an opportunity to hone their professional skills while giving performances and lecture-demonstrations at high schools and junior colleges throughout the province. Unfortunately, this minitroupe had to cease operation when LIP funds dried up in 1973. In the intervening years, however, it succeeded in building awareness of dance among a young public and in giving budding dancers an opportunity to grow.

The other outstanding work of 1970 was Nault's *Symphony of Psalms*, to music of Stravinsky, which was danced in the nave of St. Joseph's Oratory during Holy Week. For the general public, these performances had great symbolic meaning: dance was no longer an occasion of sin, but could also be one of prayer. With the church now reconciled to dance, public attitudes changed: at long last, dance was recognized as having spiritual and artistic value. Meanwhile, an unlikely crowd of dance lovers visited St. Joseph's.

In his nine years as artistic director, Nault contributed in a very significant way to the growth of LGBC. He established close ties with various American ballet companies and created works that were contemporary in style, such as *Hip and Straight* and *Aurkhi*. He made the company a popular international attraction. Finally, he integrated it more fully into the artistic life of traditional Quebec.

The Macdonald Interlude

The company was next taken in hand by Brian Macdonald, who remained at the artistic helm from 1974 to 1977. A Montrealer by birth, Macdonald came to dance relatively late. He discovered it, in fact, while studying English literature at McGill University and reviewing music for *The Montreal Herald*, an English-language daily. Macdonald studied ballet with Gérald Crevier, while Elizabeth Leese and Françoise Sullivan introduced him to modern dance and improvisation. His father, discovering Brian's interest in dance, was quick to disown him. To make matters worse, an arm injury cut short his career as a performer. Thus, after briefly dancing with the National Ballet of Canada (of which he was a charter member), Macdonald became a choreographer and director of musicals, operettas, and operas, as well as the artistic director of several Canadian and foreign dance companies. His versatility and broad knowledge of music, coupled with the eclecticism of his choreographic style, were assets that would earn him international fame.

Prior to becoming artistic director of LGBC, Macdonald had choreographed for the National Ballet of Canada, the Royal Winnipeg Ballet, and other companies. In 1956, with other Montreal choreographers, including Séda Zaré, Elizabeth Leese, Michel Conte, and Elsie Salomons, he had founded the short-lived Montreal Theatre Ballet, with the aim of promoting Canadian talent in the fields of music, set design, as well as dance. Macdonald's direction of LGBC subscribed to much the same vision. He revived the choreographic workshops instituted by Chiriaeff but abandoned for lack of funds. He encouraged young choreographers to return to Canada, a group that included, most notably, Judith Marcuse and Linda Rabin. Wooed by Macdonald, both returned home.

Macdonald had met them overseas. Rabin was working in Israel when Macdonald invited her to mount a work for LGBC's choreographic workshop. *Souvenance*, or *A Yesterday's Day*, was presented at a workshop performance at the company's studio in

Olivia Wyatt Macdonald, Christina Coleman, and Brian Macdonald in a
variety number choreographed by Macdonald, CBC/Radio Canada.

1974 and was later taken into the LGBC repertory. Thanks to this experience, Rabin
reestablished a connection with her birthplace, while the Montreal public had the
opportunity to discover her distinctive approach to choreography. Indirectly, the workshop prompted Rabin to settle permanently in Montreal a few years later.

Next, Macdonald invited Judith Marcuse to mount a work for the company. At this
time she was dancing and choreographing for the Ballet Rambert. The piece she created for LGBC won her the newly created Chalmer's Choreographic Award for a Canadian choreographer and prompted her to resettle in Canada. Eventually, she went to Vancouver, where she formed the company that she continues to direct today.

During his tenure with Les Grands Ballets Canadiens, Macdonald made two major
contributions. One was the acquisition of works by Balanchine. Indeed, the company
acquired several ballets by the renowned neoclassical choreographer, and the Balanchine repertory became one of LGBC's trademarks. Secondly, Macdonald enlarged the
corps de ballet and raised its performance standard. Under his direction, the company's
ensemble work became cleaner and more precise.

Triumvirates and Codirectorships

After Macdonald's departure, the LGBC board of directors established an artistic tri-
umvirate consisting of Colin McIntyre, the company's former administrator, and
Daniel Jackson and Linda Stearns, its former ballet master and ballet mistress. Unlike
their predecessors, none of the new directors had choreographic experience. This, coupled with the very number of people responsible for artistic decisions, mitigated

against the development of an identifiable company style and an aesthetically coherent repertory. Eclecticism reigned.

Since 1977 LGBC has undergone both financial and artistic upheavals. This has been at least partly due to the absence of a clear artistic vision. Unable to define its target audience or decide whether it was primarily a classical or a modern dance ensemble, the company experienced wild fluctuations both in repertory and in attendance.

In 1985, Jeanne Renaud became artistic codirector with Linda Stearns. Renaud was a pioneering figure in Quebec modern dance and closely associated with the artists of *Le Refus Global* group. The situation was certainly paradoxical: here was an acknowledged experimentalist heading Quebec's most established classical company. During Renaud's tenure, which ended in 1987, avant-garde works entered the repertory along with classics such as *Les Sylphides*. Although "underground" dance had a strong following in Montreal, the company's subscribers were not among them.

Despite the growing confusion, a choreographer of note managed to emerge. James Kudelka, a "renegade" from the National Ballet of Canada, joined LGBC in 1980 as a principal dancer and resident choreographer. His works of the 1980s won popular and critical acclaim. Indeed, Anna Kisselgoff, dance critic of *The New York Times*, singled him out as Canada's leading classical choreographer.[2] Kudelka remains the spearhead of contemporary ballet in Canada and one of LGBC's "hottest" tickets. A much sought

Les Grands Ballets Canadiens in James Kudelka's *In Paradisum*. Photograph by Dominique Durocher.

after choreographer, he has worked for companies elsewhere in the country and in the United States.

In Paradisum (1983), one of his most memorable works, was a deeply emotional response to his mother's slow death by cancer. The leading roles were played alternately by male and female dancers. The ballet was extremely well received. Other important works by Kudelka were *Alliances* (1984), *The Heart of the Matter* (1986), *Le Sacre du Printemps* (1987), and *Désir* (1991).

Before joining LGBC in 1980, Kudelka had taken a year's sabbatical from the National Ballet of Canada. During his leave, he attended the Banff Choreographic Seminar, an intensive month-long program that brought him into close contact with modern and experimental Canadian choreographers. After this experience, his works would represent an interesting blend of tradition and innovation. Although experimenting with new forms, he did not abandon his classical background. Intricate ballet steps were woven into tight musical phrases; his use of partnering was unusual, as was the way he manipulated groups. To his innate craft were added quick mood changes and a poignancy that made his pieces appealing to a broad audience. In the early 1990s, Kudelka left Quebec to return to his alma mater, the National Ballet of Canada, as resident choreographer.

LGBC owed its creation to the charismatic personality and dedication of Ludmilla Chiriaeff, who guided the company and kept watch over its early fortunes with the zeal of a true missionary. LGBC's birth came at a propitious moment. If, artistically, Quebec was almost virgin territory at the time, it had nevertheless laid the foundation for a structure to support professional dance. Thus, LGBC managed to survive where earlier enterprises had failed. An eclectic repertory also worked in the company's favor in those early days by nurturing a broad general audience. Today, the stakes are somewhat different, and a clearer artistic profile would help define the company's purpose and desired image.

The appointment in 1989 of Lawrence Rhodes, an American, to replace Linda Stearns as LGBC artistic director, opened a new chapter in the history of Quebec's oldest dance institution. In terms of repertory, Rhodes has pursued essentially the same course as his predecessors, acquiring new works along with more traditional ones, and often presenting classical and contemporary ballets on the same program. As a result, the company's artistic profile is not as clear as it could be. However, in promoting certain company soloists—Andrea Boardman, Sylvain Lafortune, Anik Bissonnette, Louis Robitaille— as stars, however, Rhodes has reversed a longstanding LGBC policy. He and his team have also managed—despite the continuing recession—to reduce the company's accumulated deficit and to increase audience attendance. After spending his first few years in office trying to understand LGBC's special needs, Rhodes now seems more willing to defend his artistic and economic choices.

Georges Bérard

In the 1950s, several dance troupes emerged that at least partly owed their survival to television. In addition to Les Ballets Chiriaeff, there was Montreal Theatre Ballet, which went out of existence shortly after the founding of Les Grands Ballets Canadiens. Another professional troupe appeared in 1955. Initially known as Les Ballets Georges Bérard, the company changed its name to Les Ballets de Québec when it moved to Quebec City and became the first resident dance troupe of the province's "old

Les Ballets de Québec: Lise Gagnier and Georges Bérard in Bérard's *Romeo and Juliet*. Lise Gagnier Collection.

capital." Although the company began to perform in 1955, it received its official charter only in 1959. Active for ten years, the troupe folded when Bérard left Canada in 1965. (Despite the similar names, Bérard's company had no connection with Gérald Crevier's Les Ballets-Québec.)

Bérard had been a student of Maurice Morenoff and Gérald Crevier. He then left Canada for France, where he danced in various opera-ballet companies. Returning to Quebec in 1955, he took part in *Concert Hour*, a well-known television program, as both a dancer and a choreographer. Shortly after his arrival, he founded Les Ballets Georges Bérard. The repertory was classical, and included excerpts from familiar ballets as well as original choreography. *Le Festin de l'araignée*, one of his better-known works, was first created for television and then remounted for Les Grands Ballets Canadiens.

The dance public was still small during the 1950s. Although television had introduced dance to a mass audience, few people went to dance performances, largely for financial reasons. In addition, Les Grands Ballets Canadiens had taken the lion's share of whatever market existed for dance. Thus, Bérard decided to move to Quebec City. There he built a permanent ballet company with local dancers or Montrealers. Among the well-known members of Les Ballets de Québec were Lise Gagnier, Edith (Véronique) Landory, Raymond Goulet, Pierre Lapointe, and, of course, Bérard himself. In addition, Eric Hyrst, Michel Boudot, and Michel Conte occasionally performed with the company.

Quebec City's dance public followed the company avidly. Bérard also created dances for the Opéra de Québec. After ten years, however, the struggle to keep the company afloat without an adequate support system became too much, and Bérard gave up. Exhausted, he left Quebec City for Guatemala, where he lived for a time. From there he went to Mexico, eventually becoming director of the Ballet de Aguascalientes.

The collapse of Les Ballets de Québec underscores another important fact: dance in Quebec was almost exclusively a Montreal phenomenon. Attempts at regionalization and decentralization were few, and remain so today. Only one other troupe, Danse Partout, has chosen to base itself in Quebec City. It thus represents the only alternative to the monopoly of Montreal, with its numerous companies and varied offerings in classical, modern, and postmodern dance.

Heralding Choreographic Modernism

From the Quiet Revolution to the agitation of the Parti Québécois,
the government celebrated itself by paying homage to its [putative]
allies—artists. The State needs its screens, mirrors, and stooges.[1]

The Shattered Mirrors of *Le Refus Global*

In the hope of challenging the paternalism of the Duplessis government, a group of artists and intellectuals began to meet regularly at Henri Tranquille's bookstore in Montreal. Their discussions led to the writings brought together in 1948 as *Le Refus Global*, a mimeographed edition of 400 copies published by Tranquille and distributed privately. The impact of the manifesto was sensational. Some of those who signed it, including Paul-Emile Borduas, lost their jobs; others were rejected by their families. Although most of the signatories eventually left Quebec for New York and Paris, the after-effects of their bombshell were felt in political as well as artistic circles. The manifesto shook the foundations of Quebec society and provoked a cultural awakening among French Canadian artists and intellectuals. The nucleus of a new and rising elite, they demanded that Quebec immediately join the modern world. Their challenge went far beyond the art world; attacking the system as a whole, they insisted upon a total reform of the established order.

Because the very idea of modernity implied the creation of a new order, *Le Refus Global* represented a powerful gesture for change in Quebec. The movement quickly spread beyond the artistic subculture, and within a decade, would lay the groundwork for the Quiet Revolution.

The crisis to which the manifesto alludes again and again was the issue of cultural identity, a theme with both artistic and political implications. Whether directly or indirectly, the authors advocated a strategy that aimed, on the one hand, at the "Québécization" of everyday life and, on the other, at the restoration of personal freedom. Implicit in such freedom was the rejection of established codes and conventions. In art, this translated into a refusal to embrace inherited forms or "imitate" the obsolete models of the past: henceforth, the task of the artist was to "create." Artists thus reclaimed the creative or inventive aspect of artistic practice. This quarrel of ancients and moderns was linked to similar trends elsewhere, especially French existentialism and the American "Beats."

Among the long-term effects of *Le Refus Global* was the consecration of the art movement known as Automatism. Born in Quebec, Automatism put French Canada on the international map of new art. Paul-Emile Borduas was the movement's leading figure, both as a theorist and as an exponent of the new aesthetic. Automatism called for spontaneity and stressed the importance of the unconscious in attaining the state of total openness that was a necessary prelude to creation. By thus privileging the personal, the movement represented a complete break with the past. With its emphasis on the intuitive, Automatism was a discourse that supported the idea of individuality. The initial creative response was the only valid one. No change or censorship was admitted, either during the creative process or once the work was completed. It was only a posteriori that philosophical ideas could be "grafted" upon the artistic content. Automatism thus extolled creation in its raw state. Like surrealism, which had initially inspired it, the new movement sought its symbols in the dream world. However, unlike the earlier movement, Automatism was adamantly nonfigurative. In Montreal, the two schools clashed: on one side was Borduas's Abstract Automatism; on the other, the Figurative Surrealism championed by Alfred Pellan.

The anarchic strain within Automatism was revealed by its support of artistic freedom and individual rights. If culture—including the arts—is a pillar of the nation-building process, hindsight allows us to see *Le Refus Global* as a forerunner of certain political strategies of the 1960s, when artists and intellectuals adopted a revolutionary stance and retrieved the manifesto so as to include it within the broader ideology of the separatist Parti Québécois. Henceforth, the image of the Québécois artist would be that of an intellectual rebel and liberator.

The cultural awakening of Quebec that followed publication of *Le Refus Global* was felt mainly within the French Canadian community. *Homo quebecensis* was in search of his mother culture. English-speaking Quebeckers, by contrast, did not experience the same cultural upheavals or suffer the same cultural anxieties: the cultural stakes were different. Nor did Quebeckers feel the same urgent need to catch up as did the French Canadian community, which was isolated from the rest of North America by language. The ideological disruptions engendered by *Le Refus Global* touched the Anglophone community only indirectly. According to Esther Trépanier, this cultural split or dissociation of sensibility was already present in Québécois society in the 1930s, even if a small minority of English speakers was appalled by the system. Interviewing an Anglophone of Jewish origin about her politics during the Depression, Trépanier was told: "At that time everybody was leftist. Even my mother. And you should see my mother!" Trépanier comments: "For me, a Francophone, 'at that time' everyone was a practicing Catholic, at best conservative, at worst, approaching, if not fascism, then at least racism."[2]

Virgin Births and *Danse d'auteurs*

The repercussions of *Le Refus Global* were also felt in dance. Among the artists who had signed their names to the manifesto were the dancers Françoise Riopelle and Françoise Sullivan. Married to the painter Jean-Paul Riopelle, Françoise Riopelle would make her mark as a choreographer somewhat later. Sullivan, however, was already known as a dancer, having performed with Gérald Crevier's company. At the same time, she had explored new avenues of dancemaking. Her innovative ideas were expressed in "La Danse et l'Espoir," which was delivered as a lecture in 1948 and then published in *Le Refus Global*. "La Danse et l'Espoir" is the first known philosophical text on dance written by a French Canadian. Indebted to Automatism, it denounced the obsolete training practices in dance and called for spontaneity and a return to natural expression.

The two Françoises were joined by a third dancer, Jeanne Renaud. Renaud was in New York when *Le Refus Global* appeared and thus had not signed it. However, she was closely linked to the group, and two of her sisters were signatories. These three women choreographers would become the founding mothers of French Canadian modern dance. Like scouts, they led the way into the choreographic unknown. Many would follow them.

Their work marked a definitive break with dance tradition and represented a continual flight toward the future. However, unlike music or drama, which had managed to establish the semblance of a tradition despite clerical disapproval, dance had no tradition to fall back on in Quebec. Not only had the academic dance tradition never sunk roots in the Québécois landscape; the negative attitude of the public and the opposition of the church had precluded all possibility of establishing an official school of dance. Nor was an artistic support system yet in place. Rejecting the very notion of tradition, the followers of Automatist dance now sped along the path of modernity at all costs. In adopting this course, they engendered a "tradition of no tradition." This idea, which their disciples and successors would embrace, implied a rejection of all conventional types of dance whether local in origin or imported from elsewhere. What followed was an ongoing series of virgin births, as spontaneous generations gave rise to other spontaneous generations. Henceforth, choreographic discourse would be a purely individual phenomenon. A *danse d'auteurs*, similar to the *cinéma d'auteurs*, now appeared. With its insistence on continual innovation, this movement heeded, albeit unconsciously, Diaghilev's famous words to Jean Cocteau—"Astonish me!" This would prove to be its Damoclean sword.

Françoise Sullivan: At the Gates of the Unconscious

A dominant figure first in choreography and subsequently in the visual arts, Françoise Sullivan is an artist whose work is not easily classified. At once an accomplished ballerina and a pioneer of experimental dance, a sometime sculptor and painter, Sullivan is no ordinary artist.

An active participant in *Le Refus Global* group, she pursued a double course right from the start. Initially, this took the form of a "hesitation waltz" between classical ballet and experimental dance; later, between the visual arts and dance. Regardless of genre or medium, however, her overriding concern was design in space. She took her point of departure "from life, in order to defend art, not vice versa."[3]

After studying for several years and dancing in the recitals organized by Gérald Crevier, Sullivan turned to more contemporary forms of dance. In 1944, she came into contact with artists of the future Automatist group. At the Charbonneau farm in Saint-Hilaire where they met each summer to discuss revolutionary ideas, Sullivan was introduced to Borduas's Automatist philosophy, which she quickly adopted. Applying this to dance, she laid aside Cartesian logic, substituting for it an intuitive approach stemming from dreams and the collective unconscious. For Sullivan and the Automatists generally, the artist was a medium through which images passed and were immediately reproduced in the work, a process analogous to that of automatic writing. This technique became the thread running through all her work, whatever its guise.

In 1945–1946, Sullivan visited Louise Renaud, Jeanne's older sister, who was then living in New York. Sullivan's encounter with Franziska Boas, an anthropologist, teacher of primitive dance, and early conceptual artist, proved to be a turning point.

Sullivan studied dance with Boas and organized a small exhibition of Automatist paintings by Québécois artists at Boas's studio.

Back in Montreal, Sullivan lectured on dance and contributed to *Le Refus Global*. She also produced a modern dance recital with Jeanne Renaud. Sullivan's choreographic efforts in this initial Automatist period betrayed a sensibility reminiscent of the return to nature advocated by Isadora Duncan. *Danse dans la Neige*, for instance, was performed outdoors in the rural setting of Les Escoumins. The dance was admirably photographed by Maurice Perron, whose pictures are the sole remains of a multipart project on the four seasons. Other Sullivan pieces of the time drew inspiration from jazz; these included *Black and Tan*, where the gestural language echoed Duke Ellington's teasing, sensual music. *Gothique*, by contrast, marked a return to preclassic forms in reaction to the academicism of ballet, while *Femme Archaïque* looked to female archetypes, ritual, and magic as inspiration. Finally, *Dédale*, an arresting solo danced in silence, explored a single movement gesture—the swing, which not only propelled the next movement by its momentum, but also initiated and shaped it. Streamlined, but rich in emotion and texture, the piece retains a contemporary edge both in theme and performance style, as demonstrated by the success that reconstructions of the work have enjoyed with the public.

Françoise Sullivan and Jeanne Renaud in *Dualité*, 1948.

Françoise Sullivan in *Black and Tan*, 1948.

Soon after the joint recital with Renaud, Sullivan married the painter Paterson Ewen. A period of choreographic inactivity followed while she gave birth to four sons. In the meantime, the Automatists scattered outside the country, and television made its triumphant entry into Quebec households. For a time she continued to dance with Gérald Crevier and on televised variety shows. She even choreographed a few classical works for Les Ballets Chiriaeff, including, in 1953, the first ballet in Canada on the Quebec folk legend of Rose LaTulippe, the maiden lured to death by the devil, disguised as a dancer. In years to come the story would inspire many choreographers and find its way into the repertory of numerous Canadian dance companies. Aside from her responsibilities as a mother, Sullivan used her spare time to paint and explore sculpting techniques. She returned to dance in the mid-1970s, although her involvement since then has been sporadic.

Her *Dédale* was remounted in 1977 within the informal context of a "Choréchange" program organized by Le Groupe Nouvelle Aire. The members of this modern dance company were immediately taken with Sullivan's highly individualistic approach to choreography, and several willingly took part in her later choreographic projects. It was with these Nouvelle Aire dancers that she created *Hiérophanie*, first performed in 1979, and the series of dance experiments from 1979-1980 that she brought together under the title of *Accumulations*. These pieces were performed in alternative spaces, including art galleries, Mount Royal Park, and even public parking lots, where the playing space was marked off by small, carefully placed rocks. *Accumulations* was performed in Quebec and Ontario, as well as in Italy during the opening of an exhibition of Sullivan's visual works. During this period, her work as a choreographer more closely resembled visual installations and performance art than pure dance. Her gestural language was simple and based on repetition. For Sullivan, this corresponded to her visual arts technique of "documented actions," where she herself was photographed in front of boarded-up windows or closed doors. The dance movement in Sullivan's works was dynamic in quality but also natural, with an obsessive use of repetition. As a true Automatist, she allowed her unconscious to operate freely. Her gesture derived from improvisation and directly became the set choreographic sequence.

Both in her visual and dance works, Sullivan's recurring themes are to be found in her use of the circle and in her search for the essence of pure form. She was first and foremost an abstract and conceptual artist. The purity and simplicity of her forms—whether choreographic or otherwise— existed outside time and space: they were a link between the archaic past and a streamlined, distilled modernity.

Bridging the distant past and postmodern present was extremely important to Sullivan. The timeless aspect of her work was emphasized by the idea of ritual, always present in her work. In *Et la Nuit à la Nuit*, a dance created in 1981, she turned to fertility rites of the Minoan era. Female dancers, costumed as Cretan fertility goddesses, moved across the stage in scenes evoking the cradle of Western civilization. The work received mixed reviews. Visually, it sought to portray in authentic terms the genesis of Western artistic forms. Rhythmically and dynamically, however, this search was less developed, thus creating an anachronistic rift between the visual and dance aspects of the work. The end proved to be symbolic overkill: a naked woman, seven months pregnant, walked toward the audience and set down a wicker basket full of rabbits who immediately scampered all over the stage—a fertility image par excellence!

Sullivan's fascination with ritual and her use of it in the choreographic process would find a better vehicle in a later work, *Labyrinthe*. Presented in 1981 at the opening of a retrospective exhibition of her work at the Musée d'art contemporain de Montréal, *Labyrinthe* had a woman and two men already onstage when the audience entered the hall. Veiled, the woman crouched like a sibyl over a pile of stones representing the entrance to the Cretan maze. Other rocks, laid in a circle, separated the performers from the audience, seated on opposite sides of the hall. The rock circle, a hieratic and timeless symbol, defined and separated the sacred and profane space. The two male dancers advanced in single file, retracing Theseus's route through the labyrinth. On the rocks, lighted candles provided the only illumination. The dancers' shadows were reflected on the white walls, suggesting an ancient mural or a prehistoric bas-relief—an evocation at once effective and succinct in its simplicity. Gradually, the sibyl came to life and, one by one, unwound the layers of cloth wrapped around her body like a mummy. Joining the men, she led them in a serpentine pattern to the exit—like Ariadne with her thread.

Fascinated by ancient ritual, Sullivan spent two years in Crete, living in a shepherd's hut on the outskirts of a small Greek village. There she conceived the paintings of her "Cretan cycle." The experience also inspired the 1987 dance work *Cycle*, which received its premiere during the inaugural season of the company Montréal Danse.

Innocence, spontaneity, risk-taking and the unexpected dominate Sullivan's life and work. She approached the task of creation from the vantage points of emotion and abstraction, giving birth to art objects and dance works that were both simple and timeless. Ever in search of magic and the unconscious, she offers us a vision of uncensored innocence.

Françoise Riopelle and the Dance of Objects

It was as the young bride of Jean-Paul Riopelle that Françoise Lespérance signed the Automatist manifesto. As yet uninvolved in the professional dance world, she had—against her parents' wishes—taken some ballet classes with Maurice Morenoff and a few modern dance classes with Elizabeth Leese. In fact, her first contact with dance had come from technical manuals borrowed from the Montreal public library in the hope of teaching herself the rudiments of ballet. Her real movement training took place in Europe, during the long years of her husband's self-imposed exile from 1946 to 1958 (the couple had briefly returned to Montreal at the time of the manifesto's publication). There, attracted to contemporary dance techniques, she studied with Mary Wigman, Karin Waehner, and Laura Sheleen.

Because she was a latecomer to dance, Françoise Riopelle did not pursue a performing career; rather, it was as a choreographer and teacher that she made her mark. Her first multidisciplinary experiments took place in France in collaboration with Jeanne Renaud, who was also living in Paris, her husband, Jean-Paul Riopelle, and Pierre Mercure, another Québécois expatriate. What interested her in dance was the possibility of a rapprochement with painting; hence, her attempt to create a form of "painting in movement." After returning to Quebec in 1958, she opened the Ecole de Danse Moderne de Françoise Riopelle, and managed to persuade Jeanne Renaud to

Poster for the Ecole de Danse
Moderne, ca. 1961.
Jeanne Renaud Archives, UQAM.

Jocelyne Renaud in Françoise Riopelle's *Available Forms*, CBC/Radio Canada.
Photograph by André Le Coz.

resume her career in dance as a performer, teacher, and choreographer. Their collaboration eventually led to the birth of the Groupe de Danse Moderne de Montréal, which
showcased their experimental dances on a regular basis from 1961 to 1965.

Riopelle's choreographic approach was abstract and geometric. She worked not to
express a feeling but to create a shape and inscribe it in space. Her performances integrated several arts to create an overall effect. As suggested by the revealing titles—
Danse d'objets (1960), *Manipulations* (1962), *Spheres* (1964), and *Available Forms*
(1965)—her dances were moving sculptures. Riopelle exploited advances in technolo-
gy to create multimedia performances where the gestural was of secondary importance. Images were projected on giant screens, while various geometric shapes and colors transformed the environment and even the dancers into moving art objects. The
sound score was often electronic, adding an intellectual and contemplative dimension
to the visual play of abstract forms.

Riopelle's dance language was close to the visions of Merce Cunningham and
Alwin Nikolais. Her pieces were set improvisations based on an open form or structure. Riopelle had studied with Nikolais in the United States. She first encountered
Cunningham in 1961, when Pierre Mercure organized the CBC's "Semaine Interna-
tionale de Musique Actuelle," which included a broadcast featuring not only the choreographer but also John Cage. She maintained her ties with Cunningham, presenting in
1966 a dance spectacle, *Opéra toi*, to a score by the Canadian composer Murray Scha-
effer and with Carolyn Brown, a Cunningham "star," as the leading dancer. Also in the

cast was her daughter, Yseult Riopelle, who would later dance with the Cunningham company for three years.

Riopelle's choreographic approach continued to evolve. Gradually, the abstract and plastic forms of her early work gave way to a more theatrical orientation. The change roughly coincided with the movement courses for theater students that she began to teach in 1966 at the Collège Brébeuf. With that, her collaboration with Renaud ended. Renaud went on to found Le Groupe de la Place Royale, while Riopelle became a pioneer in the incorporation of dance into higher education. Riopelle was hired in 1969 by the theater department of the newly created Université du Québec à Montréal (UQAM). There she staged performances with Mobiles, a group that she had founded with young actors eager to experiment in the then fashionable idiom of *expression corporelle*. Emotion and theatricality now seeped into her work, which gradually evolved toward a form of gestural theater or dance-theater.

Riopelle reconnected with the dance world in 1977 when Le Groupe Nouvelle Aire remounted her abstract, open-form piece *1964* on a Choréchange program. Two years later, she took charge of UQAM's newly formed dance program and incorporated dancers, along with actors, into Mobiles. Riopelle made her last choreographic works in 1980. *Tout autour et dans le fond*, a ten-minute duet commissioned for the program "Treize chorégraphes pour deux danseurs," revealed her new aesthetic concern with developing mood pieces that blended psychology, abstraction, and emotion.

Where Riopelle's development as a choreographer followed a path from abstraction to theatricality, that of her collaborator Jeanne Renaud moved in the opposite direction—from dances that were emotional and subjective to a kind of abstract art, identified with the early work of Le Groupe de la Place Royale.

Jeanne Renaud and Linear Purity

Of the three pioneers of French Canadian modern dance, only Jeanne Renaud devoted her entire career to dance. Her early training in contemporary dance was with Elizabeth Leese and in ballet with Gérald Crevier. Then she, too, went to Paris and New York, where she studied with Hanya Holm, Mary Anthony, and Merce Cunningham.

Although she herself had not signed *Le Refus Global*, Renaud was closely associated with the revolutionary movement through Françoise Sullivan and Françoise Riopelle and her own two sisters, Louise and Thérèse Renaud, who signed the manifesto. Jeanne not only embraced Automatist principles, but held to them throughout her long career, particularly the idea of breaking down the barriers among the arts. Echoing Cunningham, she believed in the autonomy of dance in relation to music. Her first works, created in France, explored an interdisciplinary approach and enlisted the help of fellow expatriates: the music, for instance, was by Pierre Mercure; the sets by Jean-Paul Riopelle.

In 1948, in a joint recital with Françoise Sullivan at McGill University's Ross House, Renaud danced *Déformité* and *L'Emprise*. Both depicted a subjective vision—the anguish and anxiety of big-city life. More expressive than formalist in approach, these early choreographic cameos revealed little interest in the linear purity that would later become her trademark. Returning definitively to Canada in 1953, she devoted the next six years to raising a family and only resumed dancing at the urging of Françoise Riopelle. They worked together on many concerts between 1959 and 1965, the year Renaud staged *Expression 65* at the downtown "pocket" theater on Place Ville Marie.

Poster for *Expression 65*. Jeanne Renaud Archives, UQAM.

The daily noontime show ran for a full six weeks, prompting Renaud to strike out on her own.

In 1966, Renaud founded Le Groupe de la Place Royale, Quebec's first official contemporary dance troupe. The company took its name from the charming square in Old Montreal where the group had its studios. As artistic director, choreographer, teacher, dancer, and company manager, Renaud wore many hats. Seven years later, suffering from burnout, she severed her ties with the company. Her career now shifted to arts administration. She became arts officer for the Canada Council's Exploration Program and then director of the dance program of Quebec's Cultural Affairs Ministry. After that, she served as advisor to the Conservatoire d'Art Dramatique et de Musique of both Quebec City and Montreal. Eventually, she joined the faculty of UQAM's dance department. From 1985 to 1987, she acted as coartistic director of Les Grands Ballets Canadiens.

Le Groupe de la Place Royale

In dances of the early 1960s like *Ecran* (1963) and *Blanc sur blanc* (1964), Renaud honed a slow, controlled movement style. Within this language of gestural restraint, the dancers moved at times to noises created by their own costumes, which variously included dresses made of wood and leotards decorated with mother-of-pearl discs. In this way, the dancers performed to sounds created by their own movements. Renaud also liked to play with line and volume, an interest that she continued to pursue after forming Le Groupe de la Place Royale.

The new company included dancers from Les Grands Ballets Canadiens, such as Vincent Warren, Jocelyne Renaud, Vanda Intini, Nicole Vachon, and Peter Boneham, who performed for Renaud during their layoff periods. Boneham, an American dancer, soon left LGBC to become the new group's coartistic director and Renaud's assistant. The company's other charter members were Nora Hemenway, Maria Formolo, and Rosemary Toombs; they were soon joined by Jean-Pierre Perreault, the first French

Vincent Warren and Jeanne Renaud improvising on the roof of Rialto Hall, 1963. Jocelyne Renaud Collection.

Canadian male modern dancer. The group rejected narrative, preferring instead a linear plasticity and an interdisciplinary approach that conformed to the principles of abstraction inherent in Automatist theory. Renaud's *Vers l'azur des lyres* (1968), with music by Bruce Mather and a set by Mariette Rousseau-Vermette, was a good illustration of Renaud's multidisciplinary approach and helped promote Quebec artists working in various media.

In addition to founding a company, Renaud also opened a school. Leaving the ballet classes to Boneham, she taught modern dance technique and improvisation, as well as experimental choreographic techniques. The financial burden of the company was shouldered by Renaud with occasional help from her husband, a well-to-do psychoanalyst. The school also generated revenue, and small subsidies came from various government arts programs. The troupe was ambitious, and by 1967 was already performing at the Théâtre Port-Royal, the smallest of the three theaters in the Place des Arts complex.

Critical response to the new group was mixed. Reviews spoke of space being constructed and "deconstructed." Renaud's approach was deemed cold and intellectual, her gestural vocabulary both diffuse and impenetrable. Being experimental, the content appeared hermetic to the uninitiated public, which failed to understand it. Finally, no one work seemed to stand out from the rest.[4]

Renaud remained unshaken by the criticism. To Jacques Thériault of the newspaper *Le Devoir*, she spoke of what the young company stood for: "an open mind to creation, a taste for new work, a curiosity always on the alert, a daring in approaches to the contemporary, these are the important qualities for dancers who want to be part of a group like ours."[5]

In addition to being regarded as hermetic, the company was also at times looked upon as "risqué." A work that earned that epithet was Renaud's *Karanas* (1968), a pas de deux that was simultaneously presented onscreen and in live performance. The filmed version was in slow motion, and although the dancers— Maria Formolo and Jean-Pierre Perreault—had performed for the camera in the nude, they remained costumed for the stage version. Although nudity had appeared onstage elsewhere in North America, in Catholic-dominated Quebec this was not the case. The Montreal public greeted *Karanas* with boos and bravos, demonstrating that it was far from ready to accept onstage nudity. A similar situation had arisen sometime before when the local "morality squad," shocked at the bare-breasted dancers in an African company performing at the Place des Arts, insisted that the women don white brassieres, lest Catholic prudery be offended. Obviously, the Montreal dance public needed educating.

Faithful to the ideas of spontaneity and unhampered creativity, Le Groupe de la Place Royale pursued its course of individual experimentation, thus prolonging the "tradition of no tradition" initiated by *Le Refus Global*. Despite the existence of an affiliated school, the creative aspect remained preeminent. In 1973, however, Renaud resigned when the government refused the company an operating grant. (Although the company had already received several project grants, these failed to cover expenditures.) Peter Boneham now took up the company's reins. American by birth, he wisely enlisted Perreault as codirector, believing that the presence of a Québécois at the helm would help ensure the group's survival.

Perreault took his first steps as a choreographer at this time. Under the new codirectors, the company strengthened ties between the visual and performing arts. At the same time, the group began to explore the use of the voice as a tool of expression. Voice classes became a part of the dancers' regular training and were also introduced into the school. After several dance experiments in the same vein, these explorations crystallized in a series of works jointly choreographed by the two artistic directors. Among the best of these collaborations were *Les Nouveaux Espaces* and *Danse pour sept voix*, both created in 1976. Boneham's own works, such as *Danse maigre pour trois voleurs*, had more than a touch of humor and theatricality. (Prior to his arrival in Canada, he had worked in musical comedies.) He also created *A Studebaker for Jimmy* as a tribute to the American choreographer James Waring, who had recently died of cancer. Perreault's works, by contrast, testified to the continuing importance of the visual arts. *Les Bessons* (1972), for instance, fell within the scope of Op Art in its toying with optical

Le Groupe de la Place Royale: Suzanne McCarry and Bill James in Jean-Pierre Perreault's and Peter Boneham's *Les Nouveaux Espaces*. Photograph by Michel Fontaine.

illusion, a trend that would be picked up a decade later by performance art groups such as L'Ecran Humain.

Despite grants from provincial and federal government sources, the company's financial situation failed to improve: its audience was still a limited one. A new strategy was then adopted: instead of conventional performances, the company would give Cunningham-style "events," showcasing works-in-progress at the company's studios and offering workshops in alternative spaces, such as art galleries. Although the company had been in existence for ten years, it had yet to integrate itself fully into the city's cultural landscape: its loyal public remained a vanguard artistic elite. Things took a turn for the worse when the Parti Québécois came to power in 1976. The new nationalist government drafted Quebec's first dance policy. Among its priorities were the promotion and preservation of the Québécois dance heritage, not only in terms of content, but also with respect to the number of performers of French Canadian stock hired for a given production. Caught between a limited audience, on the one hand, and the new government policies, on the other, Le Groupe de la Place Royale moved to Ottawa in 1977. The decision proved to be a good one. In the Canadian capital, the company has flourished, thanks to a more generous support system than in Quebec.

In departing for Ottawa, Le Groupe de la Place Royale left the field open to its rival, Le Groupe Nouvelle Aire, Montreal's only other experimental dance company. With its competition gone, Nouvelle Aire now enjoyed a monopoly of the "turf."

Le Groupe Nouvelle Aire

Founded in 1968, Le Groupe Nouvelle Aire was Montreal's second modern dance group to become officially incorporated. At first glance, its artistic mandate appeared to be nearly identical to that of Le Groupe de la Place Royale—the discovery and promotion of Québécois stage talent. However, the experiments of Le Groupe Nouvelle Aire were directed toward the development of a new contemporary dance technique that, in time, would become the cornerstone of "le style Québécois"—or so hoped its cofounder and artistic director, Martine Epoque.

The coexistence of these two groups marked the transition from the first generation of experimental dance choreographers to the burgeoning group of "independents," most of whom are still working in Montreal and who came to prominence after seceding from the two "mother" companies. If Françoise Sullivan, Françoise Riopelle, and Jeanne Renaud are the founding mothers of Québécois experimental dance, Le Groupe de la Place Royale and Le Groupe Nouvelle Aire acted as surrogate mothers to the generation of choreographers that followed. Hindsight reveals that the aims and objectives of the two groups were quite different: Le Groupe Nouvelle Aire was mostly concerned with developing a new gestural language, while Le Groupe de la Place Royale set its sights on integrating the visual and performing arts.

What was Le Groupe Nouvelle Aire's identity? The group was founded by a nucleus of enthusiastic teachers and students in the physical education department of the Université de Montréal. These "P.E." beginnings were to haunt the company long after the original members had dissociated themselves from the group. The founders included many who would come to figure prominently in dance education—Rose-Marie Lèbe-Néron, who established the dance diploma at the Université de Montréal; Gérald Fyfe and Denis Poulin, who direct the dance program at the Montmorency CEGEP; Diane Carrière, Philippe Vita, Sylvie Pinard, and Paul Lapointe, all of whom are teach-

LEFT: Le Groupe Nouvelle Aire: Nicole Laudouar, Sylvie Pinard, and Paul Lapointe in Martine Epoque's *Amiboïsme*.

BELOW: Le Groupe Nouvelle Aire: Nicole Laudouar and Paul Lapointe in Lapointe's *Mi-é-Meta*. Photograph by Normand Jacob.

ing at the college or university level. But it was mostly around the figure of Martine Epoque that the image of the company crystallized during the three periods of its existence.[6]

A Fledgling Company

Martine Epoque was a native of southern France who had come to Quebec to teach eurhythmics at the Université de Montréal. An expert in Dalcroze eurhythmics, she claimed to be self-taught with regard to dance technique. At Nouvelle Aire she quickly became the dominant figure. Initially, the group was made up of twenty-five enthusiasts who brought to dance the candor and naiveté that come only with youth. Within two years, the young P.E. students had succeeded in producing two different programs at the Place des Arts, programs made up of a dozen works choreographed by dancers and other members of the troupe. Two pieces are particularly worth mentioning: Martine Epoque's *Amiboïsme* and Paul Lapointe's *Mi-é-Meta*.

Epoque's work was the second part of a trilogy entitled *La Cellule humaine*. A choreographic cameo rich in gestural invention, *Amiboïsme* was performed entirely on the floor, imitating the molecular movements of amoebas. Only eight minutes long, the dance was a real tour de force that captured the audience's imagination despite the fact that the movement was limited to a horizontal plane. Well structured and accessible, *Amiboïsme* became one of the company's most popular pieces and was repeatedly revived. *Mi-é-Meta*, for its part, was Lapointe's first venture as a choreographer. The originality of the theme as well as its treatment astonished the public—Siamese twins in skull caps and heavy, stylized makeup desperately trying to free themselves from each other.

The exploration of a movement language tailored to a particular choreographic theme summed up the group's overall approach. The company defined its program as follows:

- to encourage experimentation and innovation in choreography;
- to discover and promote Québécois performing talent;
- to create a new technique that would not only identify the company but would also serve as the basis of a "Québécois" movement style.

The dances presented by the company during this early period were inspired by Maurice Béjart's aesthetic. The costumes, for instance, often consisted of unitards on which a few geometric lines had been painted, and special makeup was devised for each piece. Deep knee bends in second position with one foot on demi-pointe, as well as the isolated use of different parts of the torso were recurring gestures that derived from Béjart. *De Profundis*, choreographed by Epoque in 1972, illustrated this Béjartian tendency, as did her *Diptyque*, created the same year, although in this case, Béjart's stylistic traits were yoked to an ecological theme about the dangers of pollution.

Years of Incubation

The second chapter in the history of Le Groupe Nouvelle Aire opened in 1972. By then, many of the company's original members had left, and new dancers had replaced them. Although stronger technically, the newcomers had extremely diverse backgrounds: some had come to modern dance from mime or theater; others from classical ballet and even literature. Most of the new dancers held at least one and sometimes two university degrees—an unusual occurrence at that time—and they brought a questioning mind to their art. The experimentation and originality that were the company's guiding principles were now the fruit of collective brainstorming, an approach that Nouvelle Aire shared with Le Groupe de la Place Royale. However, the results were quite different. Nouvelle Aire was chiefly interested in how a dance phrase was constructed. The technique initially developed by Epoque was arduous and difficult to grasp. With time, however, it evolved, becoming more fluid and versatile, even as it retained its complex, irregular rhythmic structure, marked contrast of line and dynamics, and isolated use of different body parts.

The outstanding works of this period were *Erosiak* (1973) and *Densité* (1974, both by Paul Lapointe, and *Diallèle* (1975), by Epoque. A Dionysian bacchanal, *Erosiak* explored the many faces of carnal love. The dance style was inspired by ancient friezes, while the costuming was Roman. The dancers wore loincloths and leather leggings over sheer body stockings, thus revealing their seminudity. They moved in single file across a horizontal plane, evoking the figures in classical bas-reliefs. The highly controlled two-dimensional movements were full of silences, while other, explosive gestures released the work's underlying emotion. A male pas de deux, where the relationship between the two men could easily bear many readings, was a high point of the work. The duet could be interpreted as subtly alluding to the homosexuality freely practiced in the Greco-Roman world; seen as a duel between a mortal and a demigod, or viewed as illustrating man's double nature, at once human and divine. *Erosiak* was a provocative work and shocked the prudish Montreal audience, as *Karanas* had done. Despite its choreographic inventiveness, *Erosiak* enjoyed only a marginal success. For the first time in Quebec dance history, sexuality had surfaced as a theme. In the years to come, it would become a leitmotif of Montreal dance.

Lapointe's *Densité*, created the following year, took place in a hallucinatory dream world. Covering the entire back of the stage was a mural representing an enormous rock into which eerie creatures seemed to be carved—an impressive *trompe l'oeil* effect. Gradually, the creatures came to life. Costumed in orange unitards with attached bat wing sleeves and hoods that accentuated the hallucinatory character of their wearers, they sidled up to the sleeping figure of a woman, haunting her, cradling her, and manipulating her in group lifts. With its dreamlike transformations, the work was clearly indebted to Alwin Nikolais.

Created during International Woman's Year, Epoque's *Diallèle* reflected the concerns of the hour: male-female relationships and the battle of the sexes for power—viewed from a feminist perspective. A series of color slides recapitulated poses and lifts from the main pas de deux in tableaux that recalled Italian Renaissance pietàs. The sculptural effect was enhanced by the fact that the photographed dancers were in the nude. *Diallèle*'s choreographic style displayed greater fluidity than Epoque's previous work. Epoque's challenging technical combinations and exploration of partnering retain their interest even today.

Despite the inventive gestural language of its works, Le Groupe Nouvelle Aire was troubled by the same hermeticism as its counterpart, Le Groupe de la Place Royale. The product of neither group was particularly accessible; indeed, accessibility, as such, had never been a goal of either company. Moreover, with their diverse backgrounds and talents, the Nouvelle Aire dancers could never achieve the neat ensemble look of a well-drilled corps de ballet. Finally, many of the dancers had to earn their living as teachers, as the company had only received project grants, as opposed to funding for general operating expenses. This was not the case of Le Groupe de la Place Royale,

Le Groupe Nouvelle Aire in Paul Lapointe's *Densité*.

which had benefitted all along from larger subsidies. Nouvelle Aire was able to survive not only because of the slim profits from its affiliated school, but also—and more importantly—because its dancers were more or less financially independent.

By 1975 the company was showing signs of exhaustion. With Martine Epoque still at the helm, however, little change could be expected. Nevertheless, financial difficulties, weak management, and the need for a complete overhaul and basic questioning of the group's artistic goals combined to bring about a major shift. In need of distance and new perspectives, Epoque left for a year in Ann Arbor. The company thus found itself at a turning point. Three new choreographers—Edouard Lock, Christina Coleman, and Iro Tembeck—appeared. If movement exploration had previously dominated Nouvelle

Le Groupe Nouvelle Aire: Philippe Vita and Manon Levac in Martine
Epoque's *Diallèle*.

Aire choreography, the new focus would be the discovery and integration of emotion.
Theatricality began to seep into the company's works, and acting techniques entered its
creative process. Dances now described an inner landscape and a specific situation that
was at once personal and universal. In short, the challenge of dancemaking was no
longer to forge an innovative dance language, but to conjure with a theme or situation.

The arrival of guest teachers such as Linda Rabin and members of the José Limón
company introduced the dancers to a new vocabulary. Although the classes conducted
by Hugo Romero at his studio had made use of Limón technique, it was Le Groupe
Nouvelle Aire that inadvertently popularized the technique in Montreal. The other
important shift that occurred in 1975-1976 was the growing interest in studio performances, where an invited public viewed a work-in-progress and later discussed it with
the dancers and choreographers. These performances later became known as
Choréchanges, or choreographic exchanges. The format served many purposes: it
helped budding choreographers to hone their craft and dancers to scale their performances to an intimate setting. For the public, it helped demystify the creative process
and the dance profession at large.

The success of the company's Choréchange programs, coupled with the departure
of Le Groupe de la Place Royale for Ottawa, was a significant factor in the broadening
of Nouvelle Aire's audience. Caught between the elitism of classical companies like
Les Grands Ballets Canadiens and the tremendous popularity of jazz ballet, experimen-

tal modern dance needed to find its own partisans if it hoped to survive.

Last Generation and Disbandment

Following a period of severe financial difficulty, Le Groupe Nouvelle Aire finally obtained an operating grant in 1978 from Quebec's Ministère des Affaires Culturelles. This entailed, however, a complete restructuring of the company. Martine Epoque, who had returned from the United States in 1976, reassumed her position as artistic director. The dancers received weekly salaries and were expected to be present for the entire working day, which meant that they could not hold other jobs. Adjustments had to be made. Some dancers did not want to confine their activities to a company whose management structure left little time for experiment and favored the model of a touring and repertory company. Thus, in 1977, Christina Coleman and Iro Tembeck severed their ties with Nouvelle Aire to form Axis Dance, a collective of professional dancers and choreographers that operated as a pick-up company. By the 1978-1979 season, all of the old company members had struck out on their own as choreographers.

The dancers who replaced them were younger, technically more homogeneous, and served by a system of strong financial support. Unlike their predecessors, they had not struggled for recognition or to establish their credibility: they approximated more closely the image of "typical" dancers. However, the proliferation of "minicompanies" independent of Nouvelle Aire was by now fragmenting the potential audience for experimental dance. Within the Nouvelle Aire group itself, no new choreographers emerged. By 1980, even Epoque was forced to leave, having accepted a full-time faculty position in UQAM's theater and dance department.

With former dancer Martine Haug at its head, Le Groupe Nouvelle Aire now went in search of new repertory, which it acquired chiefly by commissioning works from previous company choreographers. Since these choreographers were also working at other venues, the repertory of the "mother" company ended up reproducing what already existed on the local dance scene. Given this redundancy, either Nouvelle Aire or its competitors had to go. Strangely enough, it was the older, established group that lost the battle. The disbanding of Le Groupe Nouvelle Aire was indirectly caused by the burgeoning number of independent choreographers, who now assumed the mantle of innovation. At once a divided and expanded territory, dance experimentation had ceased to be the tributary of its two mother institutions: it was now officially adopted by Montreal's dance vanguard. The "tradition of no tradition" surfaced anew, except that now there seemed to be as many separate creative founts as there were individuals on the scene. This proved to be a double-edged sword dividing not only the audience but the artistic community itself, which now split into factions and clans. The entire dance world exploded. Meanwhile, the government doled out morsels of aid, and the subsidy race intensified.

VI

Mainstream Undercurrents

McGill University

An Anglophone modern dance movement emerged in Montreal during the 1930s. For the most part, the dancers were graduates of the physical education department of McGill University, which, since 1929, had been offering credit courses in "interpretative" dancing. The continuing presence of dance in the curriculum was largely the work of Thelma Wagner, an American specialist in modern dance technique. Wagner held a master's degree from New York University and had studied with Hanya Holm and, at Bennington, with Doris Humphrey. Humphrey, in fact, gave a sold-out lecture-demonstration at McGill's Moyse Hall during the 1930s.

Wagner arrived at McGill in 1938 and remained at the university until her retirement in 1967. Once settled in Montreal, she founded the McGill Modern Dance Club and also developed numerous dance and physical education courses. During her long years of service, dance classes and choreographic events multiplied dramatically, creating, within the English-speaking community at least, public awareness of modern dance. After Wagner's retirement, changes took place in the curriculum, and the previous emphasis on technique gave way to an emphasis on dance education and Laban-inspired creative movement. The golden age, so to speak, of American-style modern dance at McGill thus coincided with Wagner's career. With her retirement, the impact of dance was considerably diminished.

Created in 1938, the McGill Modern Dance Club offered workshops in dance and movement exploration on a regular basis to the entire university community. The annual concerts presented choreography by students as well as faculty members, who sometimes also doubled as performers. Stylistically, the work was in the tradition of American modern dance. During the 1950s, the club began to award scholarships to promising students to enable them to take intensive summer courses with such masters as Martha Graham. This tradition continued for a good fifteen years.

Another McGill teacher was Mary Cussans (also known as Cuzanne), who had been a student of Ruth St. Denis. In the late 1930s, Cussans formed the New Dance Group. This was a predecessor of the McGill Modern Dance Club and aimed at promoting modern dance in Montreal through concerts given at diverse theatrical locales. The souvenir program for one such concert spoke of the beneficial effects of modern dance, citing the close tie between the form's theoretical ideas and actual practice, and the fact that the new medium was a vehicle for the expression of progressive ideas and contemporary concerns.

McGill University was itself remarkably progressive for the time, especially compared to its French Canadian counterpart, the Université de Montréal. Even the creation of a physical education department was a pioneering move, not only at the

Nina Caiserman. Ghitta
Caiserman-Roth Collection.

provincial level, but nationally as well. McGill also acted as a trailblazer in creating a women's section within the department. As it turned out, most of the graduates of the department's dance concentration were of Jewish origin, including Nina Caiserman, mentioned earlier. Caiserman did not remain in Montreal, however, but left for New York, where she danced both with Martha Graham and her rival Doris Humphrey, as well as with Jane Dudley and Sophie Maslow.

Despite her qualifications, Ann Naran Silverstone, another McGill graduate, was denied a position as a physical education teacher with the Protestant School Board of Greater Montreal, where an unspoken policy of anti-Semitism was in force. The job went instead to an English Canadian named Eleanor Moore-Ashton, who established a virtual monopoly on dance teaching in the Anglophone public school system. Her students worked in schools throughout the Greater Montreal region, where they taught tap dancing and ballet.

Anti-Semitism was widespread in Quebec society as a whole. Both Anglophones and Francophones showed themselves unwilling to integrate Jews into their respective milieux. Even McGill, progressive as it may have been in certain respects, had an admissions quota for Jewish students. Consequently, the place of Jews in the portrait of Montreal society is both vague and fluid: at times, they appear to be a separate entity; at others, integrated into dominant Anglophone society. At any event, Jews were an important element of Quebec's social landscape, bringing another dimension to its binational cultural fabric.

Consequently, Ann Silverstone turned to Montreal's Jewish community for a job. She was promptly hired by the Young Women's Hebrew Association (YWHA), where she taught rhythmic gymnastics and interpretative dancing. Her classes were so popular that the "Y" gave her a summer scholarship to study with Martha Graham, a gesture that revealed the Jewish community's almost astonishing awareness of new dance movements south of the border. Elsie Salomons, another Jewish graduate from McGill's physical education department, eventually took over Silverstone's job at the "Y." Of all the Jewish dancemakers from Montreal, Nina Caiserman may have achieved greatest international renown. Nevertheless, it was Salomons who laid the groundwork for the teaching of creative dance in her native city.

Elsie Salomons

Born in Montreal in 1917, Elsie Salomons was a prize pupil of Ezzak Ruvenoff, dancing in all his recitals and even, occasionally, as his partner. Salomons went to McGill, where she received her degree in 1937. By that time, she was already dancing and choreographing on her own. Soon after, she left for England, where she took classes in creative and modern dance with Kurt Jooss and Rudolf von Laban, both of whom had settled there after fleeing Hitler's Germany. Although she also studied ballet with Nicolas Legat, it was her work with Jooss and Laban that proved an enduring influence. Thus, she discovered the importance of integrating classical and modern dance techniques, a principle she adhered to throughout her career, just as she remained loyal to the idea of creative dance as a prime vehicle of personal expression.

When World War II broke out, she managed to book passage on the last boat leaving for Canada. Soon after returning to Montreal in 1940, she was asked to replace Silverstone at the "Y." By 1946 she was also teaching creative dance to grade-school children at St. George's School, a progressive institution founded in 1930 that still offers dance classes in its performing arts curriculum. Salomons was indeed a pioneer of creative dance in Montreal's English-language educational system.

In 1953, Salomons opened her own dance studio, which remained in existence until 1976. Among the dancers who received their initial training there were Linda Rabin, as well as Salomons's two nieces, Judith Marcuse and Betsy Carson. Salomons's approach to teaching was eclectic. Her warm-up was a hybrid combination of exercises borrowed equally from ballet and American modern dance techniques. After the warm-up, she had the students—youngsters as well as adults—improvise on a set theme. Typically, they had to explain to the pianist the kind of musical accompaniment they wanted. Then, they performed the piece for the group. The use of props was not only tolerated but encouraged.

In art no less than life, Salomons was politically committed. Her dances addressed concerns of the day, and she contributed to concerts given by the Montreal Theatre

Elsie Salomons teaching at St. George's School, 1946.
Elsie Salomons Collection.

Ballet and the Negro Community Centre. "5 Mount Royal West" was a left-wing Jew-ish community organization for which she organized several productions. During the Duplessis era she joined the Communist Party, thus allying herself with the Jewish community's militant wing. In 1941, she participated in a Russian "evening," choreo-graphing for the occasion a dance for peace. The social and artistic radicalism of the Jewish artistic community was well known, as indicated by Esther Trépanier's com-ments quoted in the previous chapter and reiterated in the Montreal French-language daily *La Presse*.[1]

Salomons's later choreography also had a social content. *Trial Flight*, for instance, which was presented by the Montreal Theatre Ballet in 1957, was a psychological study of adolescent angst. The influence of Anna Sokolow and Helen Tamiris was apparent in the work. Indeed, on more than one occasion, Salomons had invited these American left-wing choreographers to supervise "intensive clinics" in Montreal during the 1940s. *Ever So Very Contemporary*, a work to a commissioned score by Robert Swerlow, utilized a dance-theater approach.

Salomons's work reveals a life conducted with integrity and steadfast courage. She was the only pioneer of her generation to promote creative dance as a recreational activity and to integrate this recreational dimension into an artistic context. Today, bedridden, she fights multiple sclerosis with the same courage.

Eleanor Moore-Ashton

A Montrealer born in 1917, Eleanor Moore-Ashton was a pupil of Ezzak Ruvenoff who later studied with Ted Shawn and such noted classical teachers as Michel Fokine and Vera Volkova. She began to take a keen interest in the therapeutic aspects of dance as well as human anatomy and child psychology when one of her three children was stricken with polio and another with aphasia. By observing their motor and coordination difficulties, she developed a preschool movement learning method in collaboration with her sister, a kindergarten teacher. Her system followed the process of human neurological evolution, moving from the eyes to the head, arms, and, only then, to the legs. In other words, as a teacher, Moore-Ashton did not start with the feet and move upwards; rather, she worked the other way around.

Given this background, it comes as little surprise that Moore-Ashton was more interested in the pedagogical aspects of dance than in forming a company. In teaching she favored an approach that would lead the student to understand both the process and raison d'être of all dance activity. Halfway between dance therapy and creative dance, her preschool method was adopted in several Montreal schools after the Second World War. The pilot project took place at the Barclay School in the Côte des Neiges district. The system was taught under the auspices of the Montreal Ballet Educators' Society, which she had founded, and is still taught by former students of hers even outside Quebec.

Moore-Ashton also trained teachers specializing in ballet, tap dancing, and character dance who then taught classes in schools and other educational institutions controlled by the Protestant school board of Montreal. She believed that all her students should have a certain amount of teaching experience, even if they wanted to be performers. She held annual refresher courses each September for her assistants and young teachers in the Protestant school system, keeping them up-to-date on changes in her method.

Over the years, the classes at her Town of Mount Royal studio became increasingly classical as she incorporated elements from the Cecchetti and RAD syllabi into her method. Classroom exercises were repeated for three weeks at a time so that students could assimilate them; only then was new material added. Among the guest teachers who gave occasional classes to her advanced ballet students were Edward Caton, the dance historian Lillian Moore, and Lucia Chase, the longtime artistic director of American Ballet Theatre. Moore-Ashton paid close attention to her gifted students, even accompanying them to New York for periods of intensive training; among her friends there was the ballet teacher Thalia Mara. Moore-Ashton's most famous pupils were Margaret Mercier, who became a Sadler's Wells soloist and a principal with Les Grands Ballets Canadiens, and Vanda Intini, who danced with both the National Ballet of Canada and Les Grands Ballets Canadiens. Other former students pursued dance careers outside Montreal. Rose Ann Thom settled in New York and became a dance critic and member of the dance faculty at Sarah Lawrence College, while Zella Wolofsky performed with Toronto's Dancemakers. All fondly recall their teacher's holistic approach and her generous, enlightened nature.

Moore-Ashton worked to bring together Montreal's small dance community, soliciting the collaboration of newcomers from Europe such as Séda Zaré and Ludmilla Chiriaeff. Although she did not feel any special affinity with contemporary dance, she accepted jazz ballet, since its base was classical, and, on more than one occasion, invited Eva von Gencsy to conduct jazz clinics at her studio. Moore-Ashton was also one of the principal organizers of the Quebec Dance Teachers Association, a regional branch of the Canadian Dance Teachers Association. In addition, she was the artistic director of the Montreal Ballet, which performed at the Canadian Ballet Festival, when this was held in Montreal. The company also appeared on television broadcasts in works by Fernand Nault and Heino Heiden, a German dancer temporarily living in Montreal. Many other professional dancers, including Eric Hyrst, Irène Apiné, and Jury Gottschalks, took part in her annual recitals.

Moore-Ashton left the dance world in 1976 to spend her well-deserved retirement in Etobicoke, Ontario.

Birouté Nagys

Born in Lithuania in 1920, Birouté Nagys emigrated to Canada in 1948. She discovered dance in her native country, which she left in 1941 to study at Rosalia Chladek's academy in Vienna. Three years later, she received a state diploma certifying that she was proficient in Dalcroze eurhythmics, dance composition, solfège and music, dance improvisation, and acrobatics, in addition to character dance and ballet. She later danced with Chladek's group at the Vienna Opera House. She learned her craft as a choreographer from Chladek, who took a more structured approach to composition than the artists associated with Ausdruckstanz. Indeed, Chladek rejected the emotional excesses of Ausdruckstanz, preferring, instead, a controlled form that was nevertheless dynamic and expressive. Feeling that she had learned all she could from Chladek, she decided to move on. Her first choice was Germany, but in the aftermath of the war, this proved impossible. So, attracted by its great open spaces, Nagys went to Canada.

Once in Montreal, she settled easily into the city's small Lithuanian community and almost immediately began teaching dance to housewives at the Park Avenue YWCA. She also became a member of Ruth Sorel's dance company, where she met Alexander Macdougall, who was to partner her for many years. After Sorel's abrupt departure from Canada in 1951, Nagys continued to teach at the "Y." Two years later, she opened her own contemporary dance studio on Park Avenue. There she trained a number of gifted students, including Ina Hazen and Françoise Graham, who performed in her concerts, as well as the very young Linda Rabin.

Nagys gave her first concert at the Théâtre Gésu in 1959. Some of the works were performed to contemporary music, while others were danced in silence. She created one of her greatest works at this time—*The Song of Hiawatha*, inspired by the poem by Henry Wadsworth Longfellow. Her choreography was expressive but controlled, and based on the idiom of modern dance. During the First Canadian Modern Dance Festival, which took place in Toronto in 1962, her works—and those of her collaborator and compatriot Yone Kvietys—were singled out by Walter Sorell, the well-known dance critic who was a festival judge. Praising their strong technique and expressiveness, he described the Lithuanian artists as the only festival participants who were truly professional in caliber.

A year later, Hugo Romero, a Mexican dancer who was a newcomer to Montreal, invited Nagys to participate in a joint concert at the "pocket" theater on Place Ville Marie. Entitled *Expression 64*, the concert was the predecessor of Jeanne Renaud's *Expression 65*, which indirectly launched Le Groupe de la Place Royale. Nagys herself had appeared on one or two occasions with Renaud in works by Françoise Riopelle, but the connection never developed into an ongoing relationship.

RIGHT: Birouté Nagys in performance. Birouté Nagys Collection.

BELOW: Birouté Nagys in rehearsal. Birouté Nagys Collection.

In 1962, the Marguerite Bourgeois Institute, a French private college for women run by nuns, invited Nagys to organize a program in *expression corporelle*. This gesture on the part of a religious institution was clear evidence of the change that had taken place in clerical attitudes toward the social and educational role of dance.

Nagys made her greatest contribution to Montreal dance history as a teacher. Her open-minded approach continues to be reflected in the teaching of her former students Linda Rabin and Françoise Graham. Nagys arrived in Quebec too late to be a part of the Automatist movement and too early to form an effective company: a support system for dance had yet to be instituted. She was thus unable to make full use of her expertise or to give full return on that knowledge to her adopted country. Although Nagys remains active in the Lithuanian-Canadian community of Montreal, her professional activity is limited to giving occasional master classes at the University of Toronto and creating an occasional work for Ottawa's Ballet Classique.

Hugo Romero

Trained at the Mexican Academy of Choreographic Art, Hugo Romero was a student of Waldeen Falkenstein, a Californian of German origin who had settled in Mexico in 1940. Falkenstein's choreography was influenced by German expressionism, and in Mexico she quickly came to be regarded as an important pioneer of contemporary dance. In addition to her teaching and choreographic activities, she was the artistic director of the Ballet de Bellas Artes.

Hugo Romero and Claudia Moore in one of Romero's works, CBC/Radio Canada. Photograph by André Le Coz.

Before emigrating to Canada, Romero had danced with several Mexican companies, including the Ballet de Bellas Artes and the Ballet Nacional Mexicano. He toured Cuba with Guillermina Bravo, Rosa Reyna, and Josefina Lavalle, his partners of the time, all of whom became famous and remain highly esteemed throughout Latin America as modern dance pioneers. In addition, he danced with the Mexican company founded by José Limón. Succumbing to the lure of the United States and the American dream, Romero left for New York where he promptly enrolled at the Juilliard School of Music.

He came to Canada in 1964. Immediately, he began to choreograph, producing *Expression 64* with the help of Birouté Nagys. In 1967, he created *La Voix du Silence*, which was performed at Expo 67. Two years later, he formed Contemporary Dance Theatre at the Saidye Bronfman Centre. For some years, the company was federally subsidized by Local Initiatives Projects (LIP) grants. It toured throughout Quebec province, dancing in schools and at colleges and universities, where it presented mainstream modern dance programs based on the Limón technique. Although the choreography was not particularly innovative, it was often theatrical; in addition, the company had a consistent and homogeneous style. In this it sharply differed from Le Groupe Nouvelle Aire and Le Groupe de la Place Royale. Indeed, at the time, Romero's company was the only "mainstream" modern dance company in Montreal.

In 1974, Romero left Montreal, although he maintained his ties with the dance community. Lionel Kilner took over the company, renaming it the Contemporary Dance Troupe, and kept it going for a season or two. However, once the LIP grants ceased, the company had no choice but to fold. In the 1980s, Romero returned to his native Mexico, briefly settling in Mexico City, where he found the dance market saturated, thus making it impossible for him to form a company. He decided to move to Villa Hermosa in the province of Tabasco. There he taught modern dance classes until his death in 1989.

Passionate and fiery, Romero was known for his boundless energy both onstage and behind the scenes. His movement vocabulary was a combination of "primitive" and mainstream modern dance idioms. He choreographed several television programs, the last being his own version of Stravinsky's *Firebird* (1980), which was performed by Louis Robitaille and Claudia Moore. His most representative works were *Seascape* (1973?) and *The Immigrant* (1972?): the first displayed the poetic lyricism that was one facet of his artistic personality, while the second revealed its passionate side. Among the artists who gravitated to his company were Jill Marvin, Margaret Goldstein, André Lucas, Robert Desrosiers, Claudia Moore, and Christopher Gillis, then at the start of his career.

Linda Rabin

A student of Elsie Salomons and Birouté Nagys, Linda Rabin left her native Montreal for New York to train at the Juilliard School of Music. Although she danced with the Juilliard Dance Ensemble and other small repertory companies in the American arts capital, she gained her international reputation as an educator, rehearsal mistress, and choreographer, rather than as a dancer.

In 1968, Rabin went to Israel to work for the Bat-Dor and the Batsheva dance companies as rehearsal mistress. There, she met a fellow Montrealer, Brian Macdonald, who urged her to choreograph her first work, *Three Out of Me*. Leaving Israel in 1973, she went to England and became ballet mistress of the Ballet Rambert. The following

Linda Rabin and Dwight Sheldon in Rabin's *A Moment Sitting*.
Photograph by Linda Rutenberg.

year, Macdonald invited her to create a piece for the choreographic workshop of Les Grands Ballets Canadiens. The result was *Souvenance* (the English title was *A Yesterday's Day*), and it was so successful that Macdonald took it into the company's repertory.

Ever a nomad, Rabin crisscrossed Canada from coast to coast directing workshops and clinics in various professional dance centers. At the same time, she choreographed works for Winnipeg's Contemporary Dancers and other companies. In 1975, a project grant from the Canada Council allowed her to present an independent program of her work for the first time. The project culminated in *The White Goddess*, which marked a turning point in Rabin's career and a milestone in Montreal's choreographic history. A year in the making, the work received its premiere at the studios of Le Groupe Nouvelle Aire.

A masterwork, *The White Goddess* was the fruit of Rabin's intensive work and experiment with a hand-picked cast of six dancers, an actor, and a singer. Singled out for their performances in the original production were Candace Loubert (in the title role), Margie Gillis, and Stephanie Ballard. *The White Goddess* was a ceremonial piece involving ritual and integrating text and voice. The work's minimalism, stripped down but symbolically charged, recalled Asian art forms. The first evening-length modern dance piece created in Montreal, *The White Goddess* had a strong impact on the city's dance community. Minimalism became the fashion, along with programs featuring a single, full-length piece; the use of slow motion became de rigueur. Meanwhile, Rabin went to the Far East to study Japanese ritual and traditional theater. Asian influences, especially yoga and Zen, are an enduring presence in her works, including those that are openly lyrical and abstract.

On her return from Japan in 1980, Rabin created *O Parade* for UQAM's newly formed dance department. Set to a commissioned score by Vincent Dionne, this colorful and festive work was a synthesis of her previous approaches and ideas gleaned from her recent sojourn in the Far East. It was at this time that Rabin decided to settle permanently in Montreal.

She opened her own school, originally named Linda Rabin Danse Moderne and subsequently renamed Les Ateliers de Danse Moderne de Montréal Incorporés (LAD-MMI). Apart from university-affiliated programs, this is the only Montreal school offering professional conservatory training for modern dancers. Rabin also started a small company, Triskelian, to present her own choreography, but eventually abandoned the project in view of her many responsibilities. Since then, she has devoted her energies to training college-level professional students (with the help of her assistant, former dancer Candace Loubert) and to choreographing for repertory companies, such as Les Grands Ballets Canadiens, Montréal Danse, and the Nederlands Dance Theater.

An artist of integrity highly respected by dance professionals throughout Canada, Rabin is one of the few Montrealers of her generation to forge an international career on her own.

Axis Dance

Axis Dance marked the first attempt to decentralize professional modern dance in Montreal. The company was founded in 1977 by Christina Coleman and Iro Tembeck, who were then severing their ties with Le Groupe Nouvelle Aire. The new group arose from a desire to engage in choreographic creation, while avoiding the time constraints imposed by a burdensome management structure. Adopting the pick-up company formula widely used in the United States, the two women formed Axis Dance. A flexible and viable alternative to existing company structures, the group unwittingly inaugurated a new trend in Quebec.

Presenting three or four seasons a year, the company added more than forty original works to its repertory between 1977 and 1981. Most of the pieces were choreographed by Tembeck, the prime mover behind the group, with additional works by Coleman, Daniel Léveillé, and Daniel Soulières. Axis Dance brought together professional dancers and choreographers who wished to explore new avenues in dance theater; at one time or another, it included most of Montreal's modern dance professionals. The group's productions were funded by project grants from various provincial and federal government sources. Small-scale tours were given in Canada and the United States. The group's implicit mandate, to demystify contemporary dance, led it to perform in alternative spaces, such as art galleries, which allowed for a closer connection between performers and spectators—an approach indebted to Nouvelle Aire's Choréchange formula.

The pick-up company idea was soon adopted by other Montreal dance collectives. Qui Danse?, for instance, became a springboard for aspiring semiprofessional dance-makers, while Most Modern and Danse Cité, organizations created shortly after and both headed by Daniel Soulières, were definitely professional. In retrospect, Axis

Axis Dance: Daniel Soulières (left), Iro Tembeck, and Daniel Léveillé in
Tembeck's *Fragment*. Photograph by Frédéric George.

Dance played a trail-blazing role vis-à-vis the independents who followed, choreographers who decided to spread their wings and create companies in their own image. The collective idea thus gave way to that of a company serving the vision of an individual. This new formula spread throughout the Montreal dance community. Axis Dance was forced to follow suit. In 1981, the company ceased being a group effort and became exclusively identified with Tembeck, the company's original guiding spirit. In time, teaching and other professional commitments caused Tembeck to scale back her choreographic activity, so that by the 1990s Axis was no longer a regular contributor to Montreal's performing arts scene.

A Canadian of Greek origin, Tembeck was fascinated by ritual and by the common roots of dance and theater. In her work, she sought to create a bridge between the cultural inheritance of the past and the artistic trends of the present. Thus, her group piece *The Water Wheel* (1977) depicted the harshness of agricultural labor, while *Echoes of a Private Space* (1978), which took place in a women's prison, monitored the change in five inmates as their apathy gradually turned to tension, fear, and hate. A primitive element was revealed in *Amazonie* (1982) and *Dialogue* (1979), the latter a duet between the work's musician/composer and dancer/choreographer. Finally, *Terracotta* (1980) was a study of ancient Greek sculpture.

Modest but stimulating, Axis Dance opened the way to other loosely-structured companies, which eventually supplanted the collective's initial formula by centering on a single choreographic figure. Thus it was that the dance scene in Quebec exploded. In the ensuing fragmentation, the modern dance "establishment," represented by Le Groupe Nouvelle Aire, lost out.

Pointépiénu

Louise Latreille was the only Montrealer ever to graduate from Maurice Béjart's school, Mudra. She had previously trained at the Académie des Grands Ballets Canadiens and, briefly, with Le Groupe Nouvelle Aire. After performing for a year with Béjart's Ballet of the 20th Century, she returned to Montreal in 1975 and joined Les Ballets Modernes du Québec under Hugo de Pot. When this company folded in 1977, Latreille retrieved most of the dancers and administrative team and set up shop on her own.

She named her company Pointépiénu, a pun meaning "pointe shoes and bare feet." The name was a clue to her hybrid artistic style, a marriage of ballet and contemporary dance. Like her mentor, Béjart, Latreille believed in "total theater." The repertory of the company was made up almost exclusively of her own works. Her choreography had a zany side, as well as an abstract, geometric one: often the two coincided. With its multiple influences, her movement language was difficult to categorize. Although she declared that the solar plexus was the source of all movement, few gestures originated from the torso. Hardly any floor work was incorporated into either her classroom exercises or her stage works. However, narrative was an ingredient of almost all her choreography.

Cordes d'assaut (1979) was a psychological solo indebted to dance theater. The main prop was a rope, whose manipulations provided the work's chief movement motif while conveying the theme of inner conflict. *La Bottine souriante* (1979), by contrast, was a light-hearted group piece, fast-paced and well-structured. *Marlbrough s'en va-t-en guerre* (1978) was an excellent vehicle for two classically-trained danseurs, while *Ich Grolle Nicht* (1983) revealed a punk, New Wave aesthetic. Latreille's last work, *Evénement Noir Blanc Rouge* (1983), brought together painting, dance, and theater in a single work. The stage, cyclorama, and wings were transformed into successive canvases by the painter and set designer Patrick Fincoeur, who worked in full view of the public. Around him were the cast's dancer-actors, living sculptures whose bodies he painted in the course of the performance. Among the well-known dancers who worked with Pointépiénu were Alexandre Belin (also known as Sacha Belinsky), a former soloist with Les Grands Ballets Canadiens, Tony Bouchard, a former principal with the Béjart company, Mireille Leblanc, Louise Lecavalier, Howard Richard, Marie-Andrée Gougeon, France Bruyère, and Nina Galea.

One of the company's goals was to train versatile dancers. The Pointépiénu school, founded in 1977, was conceived along the lines of Mudra, with training in classical, contemporary, and jazz dance. Classes in eurhythmics, solfège, theater, and voice training were also part of the students' daily routine.

Pointépiénu's other main goal was to popularize dance. Thus, in contrast to Le Groupe Nouvelle Aire and Le Groupe de la Place Royale, Pointépiénu's works were seldom high-brow or intellectual in content. The company was warmly received in France and Belgium, where it often toured, because of its identification with Béjart: indeed, the repertory was more closely attuned to European sensibilities than to Québécois taste. Discouraged by the lack of recognition at home, Latreille disbanded both the company and the school in 1984. She then pursued a new career, this time in the business world.

Danse Partout

Danse Partout grew out of a choreographic workshop at the Académie des Grands Ballets Canadiens in the early 1970s, when Chantal Belhumeur, a modern dance teacher and former LGBC dancer, created one of her earliest works. The piece was well received and prompted Belhumeur to form her own company. In a challenge to the dance monopoly enjoyed by Montreal, she established the group in Quebec City. In 1976, Danse Partout became the only officially recognized professional dance company in the "old capital."

The new company did more than simply produce its founder's works. In contrast to the experimentalist orientation of Montreal dance at the time, Danse Partout ("dance everywhere" in French) aspired to accessibility: it hoped for the embrace of the public at large. Even the company's training—the dancers were versed in traditional modern dance technique as well as in ballet—went against the tide of the period. In a sense, Belhumeur had no choice but to follow a relatively conventional path, as the Quebec City audience lacked sustained exposure to experimental dance. Hence, the first order of business had to be the creation of a public that could be gradually initiated into the mysteries of a language so different from ballet. With their combination of lyricism and narrative, Belhumeur's *Siamoises* (1981) and *Rivières I, II et III* (1982-1983) admirably met the company's various goals.

In 1985, Belhumeur resigned. Like Louise Latreille, she was exhausted by a struggle for recognition that seemed to be getting her nowhere. Luc Tremblay, who had left the company to perform with the Toronto Dance Theatre, succeeded her as artistic director. In time, he imposed his own stamp on the company—theatricality and an open policy toward other Québécois and Canadian choreographers. Still, Danse Partout remains a company shunned by Montreal dancemakers. With its mainstream identity, it has little in common with the experimentalism that dominates Quebec's dance capital.

VII

The Flowering of the Independents

Dance Demystified

The "Art of Movement" Series

In 1975, in the informal setting of the Salle Wilfrid Pelletier mezzanine, the Place des Arts initiated a series of lunch-hour performances aimed at demystifying dance. Known as the Art of Movement, the series consisted of workshop-style presentations without theatrical lighting and scenery. Given once a week and with only a token charge for admission, the performances ranged from classical ballet to jazz and contemporary dance and were introduced by Henri Barras, the host of the series for many years. Attended by businessmen, city employees, and other downtown workers, the series quickly became a popular way of spending the lunch hour.

Initially, only Montreal troupes were showcased. In time, the program grew more ambitious, presenting companies from elsewhere in Canada and abroad. The formula was also somewhat modified. Although performances continued to take place at noon with Barras as master of ceremonies, they moved from the Pelletier mezzanine to the stage of the Théâtre Maisonneuve, and general lighting was added. Unfortunately, budget cuts in the 1990s caused the series to be dropped.

Choréchanges

A similar desire to demystify dance while making it more accessible inspired Le Groupe Nouvelle Aire to set up its informal Choréchange program in 1975-1976. Held in the intimate atmosphere of the company's studios, these monthly gatherings—or "choreo-exchanges"—promoted communication between artists and audiences. Works-in-progress were presented and then discussed, with audience members sharing their impressions of the performance with the dancers. For the public, these mini-performances proved enlightening about the choreographic process, while for the performers, they offered immediate feedback on their work.

The formula was innovative in that bills were shared by members of different Montreal and Canadian troupes. The series thus promoted an unusual degree of artistic contact among dancers and helped to reduce the rivalry so widespread in the dance world of the time. In a similar spirit, Jacqueline Lemieux-Lopez, administrator of Entre-Six, organized the Octobre en Danse Festival in 1978.

The very first tribute to Montreal's dance pioneers also took place under the auspices of a Choréchange event. Elsie Salomons, Séda Zaré, Ludmilla Chiriaeff, and Fernand Nault joined Françoise Sullivan, Françoise Riopelle, and Jeanne Renaud in a round-table discussion to share their memories of the past. For the young dancers in the audience this was an eye-opening experience. Subsequently, Sullivan and Riopelle were invited to reconstruct a few of their old works on the Nouvelle Aire dancers, an event that marked their return to the world of Montreal dance. Another high point of the Choréchange series took place in 1978, when Merce Cunningham gave a two-day clinic and a lecture-demonstration where he performed one of his works.

The series, which continued for five years, succeeded in attracting a new audience to dance and in strengthening ties among dancemakers from all parts of Canada.

Qui Danse?

A collective made up of rotating members, Qui Danse? was jointly conceived by Françoise Riopelle and Dena Davida, a specialist in contact improvisation who had recently emigrated from the United States. Once again, the need to communicate and to exchange ideas prompted the creation of the group. Qui Danse? brought together many independent Montreal choreographers at the threshold of their careers. The content of the performances varied enormously, as did the talent of the choreographers. Moreover, with a different group of dancemakers organizing each series of performances, audiences never quite knew what lay in store. Attendance required great openness of mind.

Nevertheless, Qui Danse? gave a number of dancer-choreographers, including Marie Chouinard and Daniel Soulières, the opportunity to create their first dances. Initially organized as a collective, the group was renamed Qui Danse Inc. in 1980, when Monique Giard, a former Nouvelle Aire dancer, became the director. The administrative structure was tightened, and in the next couple of years the organization managed to obtain a few grants.

Yet with hindsight it is difficult to regard Qui Danse? as having had an important or lasting social impact on Montreal dance. Although the group launched a few young choreographers on their careers, audiences remained small, and for all its efforts, the group did little to alter the public image of dance. Françoise Graham attempted to revive the Qui Danse? approach with her Bézébodé events of the early 1980s known as "Portiques," but this effort, too, was not sustained.

Tangente

The birth of Tangente in 1981 coincided with Dena Davida's departure from Qui Danse? The new collective was founded by Davida in collaboration with Silvy Panet-Raymond, Howard Abrams, and Louis Guillemette. The aim was to foster "New Dance" and contact improvisation, Davida's goal throughout her Montreal career, and to develop centers for independent choreographers. An alternative space for experimental performance, Tangente had a seminal influence on the promotion of postmodern and New Dance styles among the Montreal public.

Thanks to Davida's contacts with American postmodern dancemakers, many of these artists were presented in Montreal under Tangente's sponsorship. With no frame of reference for contemporary dance and little knowledge of the history of modern dance internationally, Montreal audiences were now hurtled toward the postmodernist visions of the American avant-garde, which they embraced.

Tangente offered both a venue for performance and a choreographic springboard to many graduates of the dance departments of UQAM (Université de Québec à Montréal) and Concordia University, its Anglophone equivalent. Hélène Blackburn, Catherine Tardif, Pierre-Paul Savoie, and Danièle Desnoyers all emerged from the cradle of these universities. In 1984, a second company, Tangente Danse Actuelle, replaced the original collective. More ambitious than its predecessor, the new group organized a series of national and international exchanges between major cities—Montreal-Toronto, Montreal-New York, Montreal-Paris, Montreal-Brussels. These "Danséchanges," or "dance exchanges," were followed by a series of events on specific themes. "Le Corps Politique," for instance, featured radical, politically engaged dances; "Sa Geste," dances with a feminist perspective; "Moment'homme," postmodernist dances created by and for male dancers; "Mue Danse," dances exploring new choreographic approaches. The choreographers currently active but who did not emerge from the generation of independents that broke away from Le Groupe Nouvelle Aire and Le Groupe de la Place Royale were nurtured by the activities and informal performances organized under the aegis of Qui Danse? and Tangente.

Davida's various initiatives were instrumental in establishing a communications and promotional network for New Dance, first on a national basis, then internationally. Among such efforts was the documentation center on postmodern and "New Dance" that she set up at Tangente. But the 1980s also witnessed a growing awareness on the part of the dancemakers themselves of the importance of concerted action and the advantages of establishing communications networks. Concepts of marketing and public relations as well as ideas relating to the culture industry seeped into the choreographic product. A spirit of entrepreneurship characterized the experimental dance milieu, and artists felt constrained to leave the ivory tower and integrate themselves into the society around them, while adopting the jargon that was currently in fashion. Visibility became an important asset.

Concerted action demanded new strategies. The Regroupement des Professionnels de la Danse du Québec, founded in 1984, became the official voice for all dance professionals, negotiating with ministries, the public-at-large, and various arts organizations on matters of cultural policy and artmaking. Among the goals of the association was enhancing the visibility and credibility of the dance profession and improving the public image of dance.

In the 1980s, too, another ambition surfaced: to promote Quebec dancers and choreographers internationally. The Festival International de Nouvelle Danse (FIND) was created in 1985 to put Montreal on the world map of experimental dance. With the growing recognition of the city as a cosmopolitan center of dance experiment, FIND was conceived as a showcase to present homegrown talent to producers and potential "buyers."

Originally a biennial event, FIND went annual in 1992; two years later, insufficient funding caused it to revert to its initial status. The festival's leading figure was Chantal Pontbriand, who was responsible for programming both local and imported talent. Although this prestigious international showcase brought much-needed exposure, power, and influence to the Montreal dance vanguard, there were negative aspects as well. Government grants and financial assistance from corporate sponsors enabled FIND to pay its bills; the event, however, also saturated the market. The festival began in September with a two-week marathon of experimental dance performances by artists and companies from around the world. Montreal's dance aficionados, having bought festival tickets, would then often refrain from attending subsequent local events both for financial reasons and because their appetite for dance had been satisfied.

FIND also created a virtual monopoly in terms of programming and funding. To be featured in the festival became a status symbol. However, it was not always clear why some companies or individuals kept being invited, while others, both from home and abroad, were ignored. Although some Montreal choreographers, including Paul-André Fortier, Daniel Léveillé, and Hélène Blackburn, were given international exposure, the struggle for inclusion in the festival created widespread tension in the city's dance world. Moreover, the festival diverted public funds from projects and events conceived independently.

The Dance in Canada Association

In 1973, Grant Strate, then chairman of the dance department of York University in Ontario and a former soloist with the National Ballet of Canada, organized the first national meeting of Canadian dance professionals. More than a hundred delegates gathered on the York University campus for three days of brainstorming and master classes. This led to the creation of the Dance in Canada Association, the first organization of its type and the first explicitly aimed at bringing together modern dance and classical ballet practitioners, as well as university professors and professional dance teachers.

In addition to holding annual conferences, the organization launched a quarterly magazine, *Dance in Canada*. These activities brought together the Canadian dance community, while spreading word of the organization in print. The conferences were always crammed with events. Evenings were devoted to performances by a multitude of companies from all over the country, with young talent billed alongside weathered professionals. During the day, scholarly papers were given, along with master classes in ballet, contemporary, jazz, alternative, and holistic methods of dance. These gatherings enabled participants to meet dancers from other parts of Canada and to build an interprovincial performance and teaching network.

Thanks to these annual conferences, dance professionals from across Canada were also able to assess the technical proficiency of young dancers, the range of emerging choreographic talent, and the artistic characteristics peculiar to each province. For Quebec dancemakers, the gatherings represented another way of directing public attention to their highly individual product. Moreover, the Chalmers choreographic prize, awarded at these conferences, was given on several occasions to Montreal choreographers.

By the late 1980s, these pan-Canadian events had lost much of their appeal for Quebec dancemakers, since both the Regroupement des Professionnels de la Danse du Québec and the Festival International de Nouvelle Danse had come into existence. As a consequence, fewer Montrealers continued to attend the annual meetings. Later, a new formula was adopted. This was the Canada Dance Festival, held in Ottawa, the nation's capital, every two years, between the French Canadian St. Jean-Baptiste holiday on June 24 and Canada Day on July 1. With the creation of the festival, however, the association's mandate became increasingly nebulous. The organization, which had previously welcomed all dance professionals, now began to act as an impresario for certain favored groups and individuals, performing at the festival by invitation only. This shift in intent, coupled with a growing deficit, forced the Dance in Canada Association to withdraw its patronage from the national showcase. Eventually, it ceased operation.

As for Grant Strate, he continued to promote dance throughout the country. He initiated several important programs, including the National Choreographic Seminars to help choreographers hone their craft during four-weeks of intensive discussion and creative activity. He also organized Dance Critics Seminars to foster the growth of dance writing. All these activities promoted the development of Canadian dance and strengthened the links among professionals working in the various provinces. A number of Montreal artists benefitted from these practical and theoretical seminars.

"Demystifying," "desacralizing," "disseminating," and "promoting" dance—these were the buzzwords of Montreal dancemakers during the 1980s. The ideas behind them left a mark on the dances themselves, allowing them to reach out and conquer a new public.

Toward a New Style of Moving

Paul-André Fortier

Paul-André Fortier taught literature and theater at Granby CEGEP before discovering modern dance during a summer course at the school affiliated with Le Groupe Nouvelle Aire. Soon after, he was invited to join the company, where he danced from 1973 to 1979. During this period, he created his first two pieces—*Derrière la porte un mur* (1978) and *Rêve I* (1979)—for the Nouvelle Aire dancers. Both revealed the visual concerns and theatricality that would soon become his trademark.

Fortier left the company in 1979 in order to work on his own. His first independent piece, the full-length *Parlez-moi donc du cul de mon enfance* (*Speak to Me of My Childhood's Arse*) (1979), had more than a provocative title. Indeed, it laid the foundation for the dance-theater approach that Fortier would henceforth pursue, while making him a leader of the movement that would bring a new theatricality to Quebec dance. The work marked the beginning of a major shift in Fortier's work. His two pieces for Nouvelle Aire had revealed an aesthetic attuned to the fin de siècle. His new choreographic efforts, by contrast, were almost crude, starting with their carefully chosen titles; they also employed elements of theater along with movement. Drawing on his past, Fortier now viewed the act of dancemaking through a literary and theatrical lens.

As provocative as the title of *Parlez-moi* was its accompanying poster, which depicted a bare-breasted woman standing next to a man in a suit. Yet for all the seeming crudeness of the image, the treatment of the work's sexual subject matter was surprisingly gentle, making the overall message unclear. An actor delivered a series of monologues on the sexual repression of French Canadian teenagers. The text was highly subjective, a description of the malaise afflicting the last generation of students to attend the *collège classique*. The accompanying movement expressed the theme of sexuality in aesthetic and sublimated terms. Unlike the speaker, who remained fully dressed throughout the piece, the three dancers—two women and one man—appeared in various states of undress. The impact of the work was closer to that of David Hamilton's photographic romanticism than the cinematic expressionism of Federico Fellini. The text itself referred back to Antonin Artaud's Theater of Cruelty, while the virginal decor, consisting of a padded, off-white, semicircular backdrop, evoked a cocoon. See-through plexiglass panels separated the audience from the action, forcing it to witness, in the manner of a voyeur, the troubling scenes enacted within this setting of apparent serenity. Although the work was build on contrasts, the disparity between the edgy spoken text and the plastic beauty of the setting and dancing undermined the impact of the piece as a whole.

Violence, Décadence et Indécence, created in 1980, marked a complete about-face. Where Fortier's previous work had been ethereal and "white," this one was ominously dark. The different stages in the life of a couple were clearly—at times too clearly—delineated with a flagrant expressionism. Images, at once realistic and symbolic, followed one another in a provocative attempt to shock. A bare-chested male dancer sprayed water from a long red hose on the rear wall of the stage. Phallic allusions abounded, and sadomasochistic relationships were constantly underlined. The hose, a symbol of virility par excellence, sprayed a woman lying prostrate on the floor in a simulated act of sexual penetration and ejaculation. Intentionally crude, *Violence* betrayed an urge to speak the unspeakable and to transgress theatrical and social conventions alike.

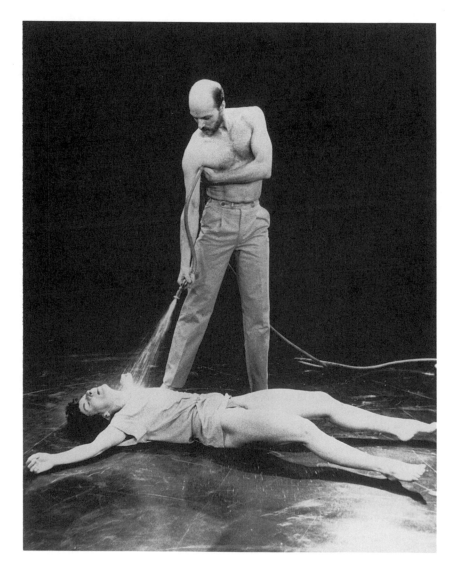

Fortier Danse Création: Michèle Febvre and Paul-André Fortier in Fortier's
Violence, Décadence et Indécence. Photograph by Robert Etcheverry.

Ever an iconoclast, Fortier created *Fin* in 1981. Here, the audience was confronted
with a Dantean world inhabited by hobos whose miseries were symbolized by rocks
attached to their necks. The image was an allusion to Sisyphus and the futility of
human action. There were sounds of kisses, and bare buttocks flashed from beneath
drab raincoats—the only article of clothing worn by both male and female dancers.
The atmosphere evoked a horde of priapi desperately trying to assert themselves, but
unable to cast off their encumbering stones. Booming fanfare music formed the sound
backdrop of the work, which marked the beginning of a prolonged investigation on the
part of the choreographer into the grotesque. Henceforth, Fortier would cultivate the
absurd, eliminating all concession to a familiar aesthetic.

Stones and sexuality are recurring motifs in Fortier's work. In *Non Coupable*
(1983), a woman wearing a blindfold was hitched to ropes with large stones at the end.
A prisoner of her own sexuality, she ultimately succumbs to an act deemed criminal by

the others—that of masturbating with the very stones she drags behind her. Fortier's profound irreverence toward the conventions of social behavior can be read as a critique of the more extreme forms of Catholic puritanism.

The leading agent provocateur of the Montreal art scene of the 1980s, Fortier was certainly disturbing. His chosen images, intended as social protest, consciously seek to provoke the reaction of his audience. As he explains:

> I place my dancers in a situation where they are forced to discover for themselves the gray, unexplored zones of my work, what is unsaid.... I confront myself with hard and provocative images, and I refuse to silence or ignore them.... I want these images to lead me to a new questioning. If this doesn't happen, I panic. [1]

Fortier's works invite many readings, while the polysemous character of his imagery lends itself to a multiplicity of interpretations. *Chaleurs*, a work created in 1985 and later renamed *Mirage*, turns on the theme of aging among dancers. The curtain opens on a scene reminiscent of Degas, revisited and updated. The women wear

Fortier Danse Création: Christina Coleman and Vincent Warren in Fortier's *Chaleurs*. Photograph by Ormsby Ford.

paper crinoline-tutus that rustle as they move. The feverish, disembodied universe invoked by the choreographer is totally fabricated and charged with heavy symbolism. Like the romantic classics that were Fortier's initial inspiration, *Chaleurs* speaks of the ephemeral and of self-destruction. As the work progresses, the costumes themselves disintegrate—an image of the "throwaway" consumer society sternly condemned by the author. The plastic beauty of the visual installation is a further reflection of the malaise that he sees afflicting today's society.

Fortier takes a similar approach in the more recent *Désert* (1989). An ecological fresco, the work has a striking design, a desert landscape lined with glass debris and other wastes of civilization. The men and women wear long, dark gray palazzo pants and move like characters from an ancient frieze. In this universe, more pictorial than choreographic, space is master and charged with symbolism. With little concern for rhythmic or gestural development, the work is closer to a bas-relief or a pictogram than to dance: it could even be called a "choreographic installation." As is often the case with Jean-Pierre Perreault, Fortier's works depend heavily on symbolic images and can perhaps best be viewed as a series of tableaux or frescoes. The message of *Désert* is unequivocal: we toil in a sterile world where the forces of nature have been annihilated.

After several years as artistic director of Fortier Danse Création, Fortier adopted a new company approach. The structure of Montréal Danse was indeed highly original, as the troupe was conceived as a springboard for local and foreign experimental choreographers. Founded by Fortier and Daniel Jackson, who had previously served as coartistic director of Les Grands Ballets Canadiens, Montréal Danse defined itself a repertory company for New Dance. At first glance, this may seem contradictory. Often, if not always, postmodern dance privileges the idea of perishability, stressing the impermanence rather than the immortality of the art work. In choosing to build a repertory of *new* works, Montréal Danse adopted an ambiguous and paradoxical stance, revealing an interest in reconstructions, even if these involved works of the present rather than the distant past.

Montréal Danse's "formula" was a compromise intended to offset the dwindling of government subsidies for independent choreographers. The company hoped to serve as an economic rallying point for makers of New Dance, who would pay the company an annual sum in exchange for producing their work. Thus, the new company offered artists from Quebec, Canada, and abroad the opportunity to present their choreography in an annual showcase bringing together avant-garde dancemakers.

Fortier's *Tell* was presented during the inaugural season of Montréal Danse. The allusion to William Tell, the hero of Swiss independence, was intentional. Choreographically speaking, the piece was a mock epic, a tragic subject disguised as comedy. The curtain rose to reveal a man standing on a table with an apple on his head. Parodic references to classical ballet abounded, beginning with the opening notes of the *William Tell* overture. The work was a choreographic collage, as well as a choreographic in-joke that recycled in a humorous way the stylistic trademarks of various Montreal dancemakers. There was the high physical risk of Edouard Lock and Ginette Laurin; the group stamping of Jean-Pierre Perreault; the ritualism of Françoise Sullivan, Linda Rabin, and Daniel Léveillé—all of whom were represented that season in the Montréal Danse repertory. In short, *Tell* was a very telling piece.

With its incongruous materials strung together in a series of non sequiturs, the work had an ironic and parodic subtext. Abandoning the grotesque element of his previous works, Fortier exposed the postmodernist strategies of his Montreal contemporaries with playful irreverence. Playing devil's advocate, he regurgitated new and old choreographic formulas with the same ease as his dancers disgorged bits of apple they were unable to swallow. The satire revealed a new subtlety in Fortier's iconoclasm.

Le Mythe décisif (1987) was commissioned by Les Grands Ballets Canadiens. The first-night audience was shocked by Fortier's openly experimental and unconventional treatment of the work's ecological theme. Danced in silence, *Le Mythe décisif* was intended as the ultimate myth, the ne plus ultra of ideology. Here, in yet another re-working of the Sisyphus myth, Fortier adopted the pose of an intransigent iconoclast and agent provocateur, come what may.

At stage left was an uprooted tree with bells attached to the dead branches that tolled each time a dancer brushed against the trunk. Other dancers ran frantically across the stage, ringing school bells that pierced the heavy silence. Two clans waged a game of tug-of-war with the tree trunk. Finally, the dancers let forth a stream of unintelligible invectives, heightening the situation's absurdity. The dance closed with a man clinging to a scaffold in a crouch, a bird of prey waiting resignedly for something to happen. Once more, Fortier spoke to the absurdity of the human condition and to the perils threatening the environment.

Le Mythe décisif was certainly not among the most provocative of Fortier's works. Nevertheless, in creating it, he made no concession to the Place des Arts public, which being unfamiliar with postmodernism, failed to understand the work. The loose structure called for some judicious editing, while programming the work as a curtain raiser was not to its advantage. Unwilling to accommodate the audience in any way, Fortier was partly responsible for the work's poor reception. The subscription campaign for Les Grands Ballets Canadiens suffered heavily as a result, thus adding to the company's financial troubles. Worst of all, the episode prejudiced the company's public against future performances of New Dance.

Daniel Léveillé

After a brief stint with Le Groupe Nouvelle Aire as a dancer of its third generation, Daniel Léveillé turned to choreography. Influenced by Françoise Sullivan, he worked from the starting point of raw emotion. This approach is especially characteristic of his later pieces, which can attain a theatricality verging on melodrama and psychodrama.

His earliest attempts at choreography centered on the theme of sexuality. *Voyeurisme* (1979) offered a sublimated treatment of the theme, while courageously attacking quasi-taboo subject matter. The piece was a solo performed by the choreographer, who moved in silence between two rows of chairs forming a corridor from the rear of the stage to the front. By limiting the theatrical space in this way, Léveillé invited the audience to view the performance as if peering through a keyhole. Lightly touching different parts of his body as he moved up and down the aisle of chairs, he seemed to be playing with himself before a privileged audience of voyeurs.

The same year witnessed the creation of *Fleurs de peau*, a dance for four men that depicted sadomasochistic relationships with great subtlety. The allusion to Charles Baudelaire's *Les Fleurs du mal* was apposite, as hints of strangling and suffocating were combined with actions of extreme tenderness. One of the dancers brandished a sword, then followed the gesture with a caress more in keeping with Paul Horn's quiet background music. However unusual, Léveillé's world was closer to Oscar Wilde than to Ken Russell.

In *L'Inceste* (1980), Léveillé dealt with the taboo subject of sibling incest. The ending depicted the union of a brother and sister, a union that bore fruit in a scene where the two simulated the labor of childbirth. The fact that the woman was seven months

Daniel Léveillé in *Voyeurisme*.
Photograph by Robert Etcheverry.

pregnant lent a certain realism to Léveillé's otherwise aestheticized and sublimated treatment.

Music by Gustave Mahler and a text by Yves Navarre accompanied the dance narrative of *L'Etreinte* (1981). Homosexuality was again the theme tackled by Léveillé: he was one of the first Montreal choreographers to explore it. Despite the nonconformist subject matter, the treatment was highly romantic: the male duet, for instance, stressed the quality of tenderness, even if it was performed in the nude. Flashes of realism cut into the work's neoromanticism: at one point, a real cat cleaned itself while perched on the back of a dancer; at another, a dancer mangled his partner with a bouquet of long-stemmed red roses. In dwelling on sexuality such works bear comparison with Fortier's. The theme, so evident in dance works of the late 1970s, reflected the legacy of centuries of sexual repression in Quebec. However, the once taboo subject tended to be treated poetically, as though observed through a soft-focus magnifying lens.

Léveillé's neoromantic approach eventually gave way to a more theatrical one. In his frequent collaborations with theater people, he saw his role as that of a catalyst, a transmitter-receiver of the actors' improvisations. His recurring themes—personal loneliness, unrequited love, the difficulty of human communication—linked him to the dance-theater tradition of Pina Bausch. *Jericho*, produced in 1986 by Montréal Danse, exemplified the tendency toward histrionic exaggeration that he now favored.

In *Mémoires d'un temps ravagé*, created in 1988 for the UQAM dance department,

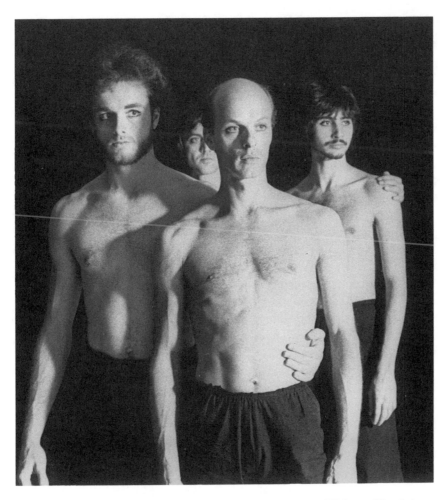

Stéphane Comtois, Gilles Simard, Paul-André Fortier, and Edouard Lock in
Daniel Léveillé's *Fleurs de Peau*. Photograph by Robert Etcheverry.

Léveillé returned to minimalism: emotion was conspicuously absent. The forty-five-minute work hammered home the metaphor of the title, which translates as "Memoirs of a Ravaged Time." Some twenty dancers, crouched in staggered lines on a stage stripped of wings and covered with a fine white powder, repeated over and over again the gesture of dusting the floor.

As the piece progressed, the cloud of dust gradually reached the audience, which felt momentarily asphyxiated. The scene evoked the dusty attic of individual or collective memory, an impression reinforced by the fragments of classical music played off-stage by a dancer-pianist. When the performers were not busy "dusting," they faced the back wall, jumping tirelessly in place or stamping fiercely. A sense of futility and immense solitude pervaded this visually minimalist and emotionally draining piece. Bordering on nondance and conceptual art, *Mémoires* was a harrowing meditation on the futility of all human action.

As dancemakers, Fortier and Léveillé are intentionally disturbing. Whether acting as agents provocateurs or enfants terribles, they give their audiences shock treatments through the content and form of their works. Committed artists, they use dance as an instrument of social protest and a vehicle of total artistic freedom.

Edouard Lock

Edouard Lock first attracted public attention with *Tempsvolé*, created in 1976 for Le Groupe Nouvelle Aire. Strange as it may seem today, this first piece of his was lyrical and full of feeling, depicting with skill and humanity a classic love triangle: unsurprisingly, it quickly became an audience favorite. By contrast, *La Maison de ma mère*, his next piece for Nouvelle Aire, was dark and charged with neoexpressionist symbolism. The work was an inner voyage, a recollection in all likelihood of the artist's own past, that also touched on themes of alienation and melancholy. In retrospect, *La Maison* can be seen as a forerunner of the neoexpressionist dance theater so popular with Montreal choreographers in the years that followed. In these two works, Lock exposed the fragility of human relationships with an emotional intensity comparable to cinema verité. In his "dance verité," the hyperrealism of the situations proved disturbing to audiences unprepared for such an approach.

Lock created two other pieces for Le Groupe Nouvelle Aire—*Remous* (1977) and *Le Nageur* (1978). Both displayed a new and extreme aesthetic that stylistically evoked the decadence of the fin de siècle. But it was *Lily Marlène dans la Jungle* (1979), Lock's first work as an independent, that proved a harbinger of his future trademark style. Beginning with the evening-long *Lily Marlène*, he adopted the rule of presenting no more than one work on a program. His compositional method was based on cinematic montage, a technique that he had studied in film courses at Concordia University. All the elements, from the dance variations to the images, were meticulously assembled into the final work. The thematic treatment was lighter than before and influenced by dada, with sequences stitched together alogically. He borrowed equally from tap and Indian mudras, while also including steps from ballet and modern dance. Images were turned into caricatures that had to be performed frenetically. With *Lily Marlène*, Lock introduced the variety show format that he still favors, with minor costume changes for each of the individual numbers. T-shirts were the basic costume, and as the dance progressed, they were splattered with paint and covered with scribbles or *X*s.

The same dadaist approach appeared in *Oranges, or the Search for Paradise* (1981). The work offered a series of cityscapes made of papier-mâché and paper walls decorated with graffiti. *Oranges* marked a choreographic breakthrough for Lock. For the first time he explored the element of physical risk, asking the dancers, for instance, to balance precariously on top of a neat row of old milk bottles. The work revealed the social neurosis of a "disposable" civilization and increasingly fast-paced life. Gestures were accumulative and performed at high speed. The score, created onstage by the young Michel Lemieux, was electrifying. Enigmatic messages were scrawled on the paper walls, which served as giant note pads. There was a hand dance performed in gloves, another based on spasms and ticks, and a third consisting solely of falls. Already, Lock was exploring a new movement lexicon, one that he would subsequently theatricalize. His approach had much in common with the punk and new wave aesthetic.

His next piece, *Businessman in the Process of Becoming an Angel* (1983-1984), continued this gestural exploration. Here he grafted everyday and functional movement onto an electronic score. Phrases were speeded up, chopped up, or both. Dance sequences were broken down and reassembled in an infinite variety of combinations. The Edouard Lock style was born. Mathematical and precise, wild, zany, and poker-faced, it integrated the principles of framing and montage borrowed from film. Repetitive but with multiple variants, progressive but lacking closure, Lock's works can last for ten minutes or go on for two hours.

ABOVE: La La La Human Steps: Louise
Lecavalier and Marc Béland in Edouard
Lock's *New Demons*.

RIGHT: La La La Human Steps: Louise
Lecavalier and Marc Béland in Edouard
Lock's *New Demons*. Photogragh by Edouard
Lock.

Lock also made use of advanced production techniques, which he exploited in his staging. Increasingly multidisciplinary, his works were close to musical theater. A major turning point came when he changed the name of his company from Lock-Danseurs to La La La Human Steps, thus linking the group to new wave rock and the latter's concert network. Abandoning expressionism and the social critique of his older works (although not their contemporary look), he now embraced a more popular style accessible to a broader audience.

In *Human Sex* (1985), he combined video clip effects with a clearer subtext. At the time an androgynous look was in style in Montreal, as elsewhere. Putting gender differences aside, he neutered the images and roles of his men and women dancers: henceforth, they would be solely human creatures. The work reversed gender roles. Louise Lecavalier, the female lead, wore a fake moustache, while her partner, Marc Béland, was outrageously made up à la Boy George. Nautilus training had done wonders for Lecavalier, and with his daredevil performers Lock now worked to forge a new movement language.

Starting from the premise that all movement eventually "dies," Lock refused to ignore the pull of gravity. Instead of soaring, his dancers made high-speed crash landings—the very antithesis of ballet's thirst for the airborne. The final image of *Human Sex* was especially memorable: Béland rushed back and forth across the stage, hurled himself into the arms of his partner, who lifted him overhead, then threw him to the floor. A bionic woman without the aid of steroids, Lecavalier revealed a new image of herself, that of a woman who stops at nothing.

As used by Lock, the human body became a sounding board for androgynous, primal energy. There was a sustained exploration of jumps executed horizontally and ending in a headlong fall. It was this moment rather than the preceding jump that Lock chose to underscore. Breakdancing also left a mark on his approach, which disguised the theme of punk *mal de vivre* under a veneer of high physical risk and superhuman prowess. Lock packaged his aerobics in the style of comic-book caricature and pushed the cardiovascular system to the very limits of the possible—all in reaction to the minimalism then dominant in Montreal dance.

In *New Demons* (1987), Lock adopted a transcultural scenario. Ballet steps were appropriated and then distorted to update their style. Traditional Indian music and Western rock rhythms were spliced into the score, and the staging incorporated high-tech gadgetry. The result was a hybrid mix of retrieved cultural and historical forms that went well beyond the discoveries of *Human Sex*. In both cases, the action moved forward in fits and starts, spasms, and short bursts. These "flash" sequences were then edited together like the shots of a film. Lock's "heavy metal" dance style was "hot" and "in," at once spectacular and virtuosic.

The shift toward a more marketable commodity took place sooner rather than later in Lock's career, with the hermetic symbolism of his early works giving way to a fast-food, more popular type of recipe. His overcharged and perilous medium has become his main message.

Ginette Laurin

A remarkable dancer, Ginette Laurin has performed for nearly all of Montreal's independent choreographers. She turned to choreography after leaving Le Groupe Nouvelle Aire and is the only woman among the New Dance choreographers who emerged from that company. Her movement is fast-paced and often teasing. O Vertigo, her company, alludes to the giddiness and loss of balance that she pursues with seeming casualness.

Laurin's choreographic sensibility differs from that of the dancemakers with whom she has worked. She sprinkles her pieces with humor and reminds us of her beginnings as a gymnast by the athleticism of her dance phrases. These demand high energy and a physical risk comparable to that of high-wire artists. Laurin mocks social stereotypes more lightly than Fortier or Léveillé and with greater humor than Lock. Her social commentary is lively rather than somber and expressionist. Moreover, she is intent on crafting a new movement language, a personal idiom adequate to the needs of form and content alike.

In some of her works, including *Tango Accelerando* (1987), commissioned by Les Grands Ballets Canadiens, she creates movement phrases consisting of steps linked together in unusual ways. In *Tango*, for instance, the couples perform the traditional figures of the dance lying on the floor. Unfortunately, the piece fails to develop, while its spatial and design elements remain unintegrated into the choreography. *Olé*, a comic duet danced around a chair, is a another, more successful tango work.

In *Timber* (1986), an earlier piece, Laurin had examined both the phenomenon of the fall and the fear inherent in the act itself. She brought a psychological dimension to the theme, and to the physical risks involved in losing balance. *Timber* was a pièce de résistance that synthesized all of Laurin's previous explorations and held the audience spellbound for the entire ninety-minute performance. The action took place in a fragmented space: the dancers vaulted at the edge of scaffolds of varying heights, before tumbling into the void. To meet the technical demands of the piece, minimize the risk of injury, and master their fear, the dancers took acrobatics classes. In *Timber*, Laurin pushed Doris Humphrey's principle of fall and recovery—the "arc between two deaths"—several steps further. The suspense left audiences both fascinated and troubled.

From Risqué Subject Matter to High Physical Risk

Lock's audiences, too, experienced these vicarious thrills. If Quebec dance of the late 1970s revealed a partiality for "risqué" or daring subject matter, the trend of the 1980s was toward high physical risk, as seen in the work of Laurin and Lock. Both courted risk, pushing the body to the limits and extracting performances from the dancers that were nothing short of astonishing. Although shaking audiences from their apathy, the provocation of these two choreographers is quite different in its impact from that of Fortier or Léveillé.

Danger and physical risk are not the only creative elements of Laurin's choreography. Some of her works display a high degree of movement invention as well as a skillful and unusual use of props. The 1986 *Chevy Dream* brought onstage a genuine powder-blue Chevrolet of the 1950s, complete with chrome trimmings and tail fins. The action took place in, around, and on top of the car, poking fun at the generation that grew up on the television series *Happy Days*.

As the curtain rose, the headlights glared at the audience. A man turned on the car, then opened the trunk: Laurin emerged, wearing sneakers, short socks, a miniskirt, and striped panties. The comic sequences that followed were danced on the hood. A gust of wind from a portable fan allowed occasional glimpses of her muscular thighs and her powder-blue panties. Although pleasant and impeccably danced, *Chevy Dream* was a light piece with neither the depth or impact of *Timber*.

Chagall (1989), by contrast, was inspired by an exhibition of the painter's work in Montreal. Thanks to Laurin's extensive research, his febrile dream world was admirably translated in her choreography. A colorful, childlike universe, full of innocent fantasy, opened before the audience. However, just as in the canvases that were the choreographer's inspiration, the work lacked development, lingering over the spatial component and neglecting the evolution of the work in time.

In her search for contrasts and the unexpected, Laurin is close to other Montreal choreographers of her generation. Her experiments with equilibrium are done with seeming casualness. Small women dancers lift tall men as if this were the most natural thing to do. Roles are often reversed, and the expectations of the audience challenged.

Laurin's work is as rich and diverse as her personality. She is both funny and serious, and she plays with danger no less than craziness with an ease that sets her apart

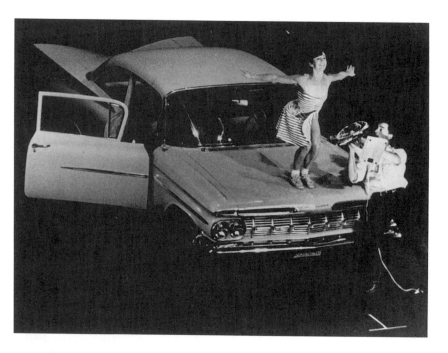

ABOVE: O Vertigo: Ginette Laurin and Kenneth Gould in Laurin's *Chevy Dream*. Photograph by Guy Palmer.

LEFT: O Vertigo: Nathalie Morin and Alain Gaumond in Ginette Laurin's *Chagall*. Photograph by Christine Guest.

from her colleagues. Finally, Laurin and Lock are the only Montreal dancemakers bent on developing a movement idiom that is inventive and intensely personal, so much so that critics, at a loss to define it, have simply called it *"le nouveau bouger montréalais"*—"Montreal's new way of moving."

Jean-Pierre Perreault

Jean-Pierre Perreault is the only prominent choreographer of this generation who emerged from Le Groupe de la Place Royale. He is also Montreal's first homegrown male modern dancer. He studied ballet and contemporary dance at the Place Royale school, then trained in New York with Merce Cunningham and James Waring. A trip to Asia, where he discovered Javanese and Balinese dance styles, completed his dance education.

After dancing with Le Groupe de la Place Royale, he began to choreograph for the company, eventually becoming its artistic director. From the start, he espoused the group's Automatist principles, especially the idea of open collaboration between the performing and visual arts, a loyalty reflected in *Les Bessons* (1972), his first work. Here, as in his subsequent choreography, Perreault created a gestural world that was uniquely his own, while also searching to create a theatrical space appropriate to the piece at hand.

Many of Perreault's movement ideas drew their inspiration from the Far East, including the broken wrist lines, flexed feet, and deep knee bends in second or fourth position often seen in Asian dancing. But he stripped such movements of their "sacred" status, using them as everyday, vernacular elements.

After exploring the use of voice as a choreographic tool in his joint work with Peter Boneham, Perreault began to give increasing importance to the visual element in his productions. Movement invention ceased to be a dominant concern. Simple steps were repeated, along with poses and stereotypical gestures. In his development as a choreographer, however, Perreault revealed an ever greater rhythmic complexity.

After incorporating voice into his pieces, Perreault turned his attention to the performer, whom he now defined as a one-man orchestra creating the sound accompaniment of a dance. This was not a new idea: Mary Wigman and others had made similar experiments in freeing dance from the tyranny of music. In Perreault's case, however, the step revealed the influence of Cunningham and John Cage, who insisted upon the autonomy of the arts even within a framework of collaboration.

Perreault's collaboration with the Vancouver composer David MacIntyre was a milestone in his career. In *Refrain: An Opera* (1980), to which MacIntyre contributed not only the music but also the scenario, Perreault accepted the challenge of choreographing a group piece for nondancers in an experimental production at Simon Fraser University. This was the first time that Perreault had worked with large groups and also the first time that he used overalls as costumes. Here, too, he explored the possibility of using the performers (who were wearing clogs) to stamp out the rhythms of the music with their feet. Acting on another of MacIntyre's suggestions, he had the actors play the harmonica, which was a novelty at the time.

Perreault would return to this strategy and employ it to better effect in a work for Le Groupe de la Place Royale that was also composed by MacIntyre. *Calliope* (1981) integrated music and movement in the same performer: the tuxedoed men and women not only danced, but also played the harmonica, sometimes performing the two actions simultaneously. If *Refrain* had sown the idea, *Joe* (1983) would reap the harvest of the intervening years of experiment. *Dernière Paille* (1977), a collaboration with Sandra

Neels, had previously awakened his interest in unisex costuming. In blurring gender and personality differences among the performers, Perreault saw a way of banishing emotion and emphasizing pure form. The installation of *Dernière Paille* included ramps, which also became an integral part of his later work.

The rhythmic concerns that first surfaced in *Refrain* became clearer in later works. He discovered the richness of vernacular movement and simplified both his lines and gestures. Music became contextual, with hammering rhythms that amplified and colored the movement, excessively so in some cases, creating a dance of exaggerated expressionism. Perreault emphasized to the point of obsession his visual, gestural, and rhythmic motifs in a prolonged ostinato.

When choreographing dances without the crutch of music, Perreault invested the dance phrase itself with rhythmic complexity. Amplified by silence, the steps were "hammered" to enhance their articulation. Boots were added. Later, the floor would be "prepared" by placing microphones underneath prefabricated sheets of plywood, so as to magnify the sound of the dancers' movements. The floor thus became a sound chamber or enormous drum echoing the dancers' rhythms. This type of experimentation reached a climax with *Joe*, which Perreault created after leaving Le Groupe de la Place Royale. Wearing bowler hats, raincoats, and army boots, the twenty-four men and women danced a paean to the squalid existence of Everyman.

Using the framing technique of cinema, Perreault summoned to the stage images of

The Fondation Jean-Pierre Perreault in the 1989 version of Perreault's *Joe*.
Photograph by Robert Etcheverry.

the suppressed individual. A tide of standardized humanity moved across the stage—panic-stricken victims of the Great Depression, scarecrows, ravens. Pounding feet conveyed the isolation of the individual caught up in the steamroller of the majority. The few moments of calm were punctuated by the notes of a solitary harmonica player. With *Joe*, Perreault entered an oppressive and depersonalized universe, while bringing a critical eye to bear on society at large. Indeed, *Joe* conjures up the worlds of George Orwell and Franz Kafka. The message of this ninety-minute work was nothing less than scathing: anonymity is man's fate.

Joe was followed by *Stella* (1985). Intended as a female counterpart to *Joe*, it met with a lukewarm reception: Perreault's mass groupings were already familiar, while the female world that *Stella* invoked was less than fully convincing. The real innovation of the work lay in its scenic design, which was striking. Pyramids of various heights filled the stage, along with ramps where troops of women marched in formation—images that recalled not only the constructivist films of Sergei Eisenstein, but also fascism. The women in *Stella* were pawns of society. Yet as a study of the female condition, the work fell short. Neither feminist nor antifeminist in intent, *Stella* had more than a touch of machismo.

Perreault's next piece, *Eldorado* (1987), also used pyramids and ramps, although their scale was reduced. The cast was pared down to eight dancers, and the action condensed to twenty minutes. With its smaller scale and emphasis on the horizontal plane,

The Fondation Jean-Pierre Perreault in Perreault's *Stella*.
Photograph by Robert Etcheverry.

the decor produced a meditative effect rather than an impression of monumentalism. Emotion was banned. Instead, Perreault focused on manipulating the movement material so as to explore every aspect of a theme. Like many of his works, *Eldorado* came to an end when all the possible variables had been worked out.

Nuit (1986), on the other hand, stretched perceptions of three-dimensionality and stage perspective. Acting as an architect of choreographic space, Perreault shifted the incline—or rake—of the stage, so that the side closest to the audience was higher, rather than lower. Thus, the usual perspective was distorted: the audience viewed the action as if lying on the floor. More common in the visual than performing arts, the device underscored the meaning of perspective.

The step vocabulary borrowed from flamenco heel work and tap rhythms. The action took place in a twilight world, which further accentuated the isolation of the eight people and the absence of genuine communication among them. *Nuit* issued from the choreographer's desire to humanize his stage characters. Yet despite the presence of greater intimacy, the work conveyed little more than the anonymity and futility of human life, just as Samuel Beckett had described. Visually, choreographically, and thematically, *Nuit* was austere.

Highway 86 was a dance event created by Perreault on the site of Vancouver's World's Fair. This was not the first time he had choreographed a work for outdoor performance. While still a member of Le Groupe de la Place Royale, he had created *Les Dames aux vaches* (1978), a series of female solos performed on a lawn with grazing cows. But the highway he now chose as his site was filled with trucks, jeeps, and motorcycles that had all been painted gray so as to blend into the road. The public, which included ordinary Fair visitors, watched from the sides of the highway.

Some fifty dancers, all in *Joe*'s trademark costumes, took to the highway. Like *Joe*, *Highway 86* sought an architectural perspective. However, the cluttered space where the work was performed, the proximity of the audience, and the monorail passing overhead, could not duplicate the conditions of the theater. The audience was distracted. Moreover, the many vehicles crowding the highway blocked the way of the dancers.

The slow, successive images—like a series of still photographs—had none of the impact they would have had in a theater. The gestural and spatial organization was lost in the vast urban environment. Moreover, the vacationers who made up most of the audience were unfamiliar with experimental choreography and appreciated neither the minimalism of the work nor Perreault's concern for architectural volume.

In works like *Joe*, Perreault poses as a master builder, a "sceno-choreographer" subordinating the different aspects of the whole to a single, overriding idea. In turning to the visual arts for inspiration, he reveals the legacy of Le Groupe de la Place Royale. If Perreault seems at times to quote himself, he also continues to explore. Working with a minimum of choreographic tools, he has perfected the art of the variation. Whereas the impact of Fortier's work lies in the razor-sharp delivery of a social message, that of Perreault's lies in painting the abstract image of a mood within an expressionist-style design. His works are urban visions of society—raw, meticulously crafted, and powerful.

With the community for both mainstream and experimental dance so much better organized than before, the most recent generation of choreographers to emerge in Montreal
has escaped the tribulations of its predecessors. Nerve centers such as Tangente Danse
Actuelle, Danse Cité, and Danséchanges now exist to shoulder at least part of the burden of creating new forms of dance. Despite the existence of structures for marketing
New Dance, however, it would be naive to think that this has achieved legitimacy in the
eyes of the public at large, which remains, as ever, indifferent. Faced with the proliferation of young choreographers and the fragmentation of the dance scene, each dance-
maker has cultivated a small audience of followers, thereby dividing the dance world
even more, while failing to gain widespread acceptance.

The three choreographers who are discussed in this chapter cannot really be considered leaders of the young emerging generation, nor can they be included with Lock,
Perreault, Fortier, or Léveillé, since their breakthrough as artists took place slightly
later. Crafting their works in isolation, each brings a distinctive personality to the landscape of experimental dance in Montreal.

Michael Montanaro

Born in the United States, Michael Montanaro returned to Montreal after a ten-year
career with Le Groupe de la Place Royale, first in Montreal and then in Ottawa. Prior
to this, he had participated in the last season of Les Compagnons de la Danse, the
small touring company affiliated with Les Grands Ballets Canadiens.

In 1985, he followed the growing trend and began to work independently. He chose
to settle in Montreal, where a productive period in his career now opened. He participated in Tangente's "Moment'homme," as well as its "Montreal-Paris" series, and took
part in the first Festival International de Nouvelle Danse. He formed a company, Montanaro Danse, which was selected to tour under the auspices of RIDEAU (Réseau
indépendant d'événements artistiques unis) and CINARS (Comité international des
arts de la scène), organizations promoting Quebec culture. National and international
tours followed provincial ones.

Montanaro stood on the periphery of the dominant trends in Quebec experimental
dance. Nevertheless, from the start, he benefited from the support structure and exposure of alternative spaces. The existence of these structures within programs of cultural
exchange fostered interest in young choreographers, while providing them with some
sort of initial government support.

In many respects, Montanaro's career has always been somewhat unusual. Trained
in musical theater and ballet in Boston, he discovered modern dance at Le Groupe de

la Place Royale. His choreography is an amalgam of musical, visual, theatrical, and movement influences. Fully conversant with music, he works with equal ease in mainstream and experimental dance idioms, and translates his interest in theatricality into an extensive use of video and film. Faithful to the Place Royale aesthetic, he aims at fusing the different media into a fully integrated work that is the fruit of an across-the-board investigation.

Like Perreault, Montanaro privileges the concept of "total" theater. While still a member of Le Groupe de la Place Royale, he was the first to experiment with a movement idiom based on stamping and foot rhythms—actually, a modified version of tap dancing, which he had previously studied. Like a Renaissance man, he displays a multiplicity of talents, creating film scenarios, designing some of his own sets, and even composing the electronic music for some of his works.

Montanaro's productions bear a certain kinship to those of La La La Human Steps in their dadaist and surrealist approach and in their choreographic treatment. Their impact, however, is quite different from that of works more typical of the Montreal avant-garde.

In his wish to heighten the theatrical aspect of his works, Montanaro calls on

Michael Montanaro: Integrated Media: Mireille Demerse (left), Simon Alarie, and Maryse Carrier in Montanaro's *Un temps perdu de Zman Doe*. Photograph by Chris Randle.

humor, thus distancing himself from the expressionist *angst* and austerity of other Montreal choreographers. His multidisciplinary works are the result of an arduous two-year incubation and are only presented when they are ready: he does not believe in showing works-in-progress. Experiment takes place in advance and behind closed doors. As in *Théories des théories* (1987), Montanaro's movement is complex, rigorous, and innovative. At the same time, it is never hermetic. Accessible, "transdisciplinary," and technically sophisticated, his works thus fill a curious slot, one with negative as well as positive consequences. Whereas Quebec and Canadian producers see him as an innovative artist acceptable to the general public, he is viewed by some of his peers as leaning toward the more commercial and accessible forms of dance.

His evening-long work *Un temps perdu de Zman Doe* (1989) successfully integrated electronic media and movement exploration in a grand urban fresco. Using video clips in a rush of "flash" images, Montanaro created a sensory, audiovisual kaleidoscope. The piece opens with a heckling Superman, portrayed here as a seated rag doll with a missing arm and a bandaged head, closer to a reworked image of the Invisible Man than to the comic strip hero. A pseudo-documentary slide show follows—a succession of "clips" of past and current events in today's global village. A message announces that the piece has no message, but should be taken as a fairy tale. Thus begins the fascinating journey through Montanaro's richly endowed futurist imagination via a design that plays havoc with the audience's perceptions of space.

First performed in a warehouse in Montreal's old port, the piece used dissolves to fade between the dream world and reality. The dancers moved in and out of a trompe l'oeil cardboard architecture that distorted perspective and shattered the space. The timing was extremely precise. Gestures were disjointed, borrowed from the sign language of deaf-mutes and traffic policemen. The dancers explored a seemingly infinite variety of body combinations with a sense of play and using movements that were both lyrical and highly physical.

Despite the announcement that no moral was intended, the combination of the set's distorted perspectives and the fragmented images of contemporary society charged the subtext with meaning. The senses were assaulted from all sides. The dancing, too, was seductive. *Un temps perdu de Zman Doe* was certainly accessible. But it was also extremely sophisticated—at once a monument to the past and a harbinger of trends to come.

Marie Chouinard

Right from the start of her career, Marie Chouinard has cultivated and projected a public image of herself as the enfant terrible of Montreal dance. Although she briefly trained with Michel Conte and Tom Scott at the Studio d'expression corporelle, she is largely self-taught. An anarchist, she calls herself an "artist of the body," understanding dance in the broadest sense of the word. In time, she was accepted by the public, despite the iconoclasm that often marked her early work. Her acceptance reveals a change in public attitudes in Quebec and in Canada at large: today, "marginal" artists can pursue careers off-limits to previous generations.

Chouinard's Canadian reputation was quickly established after presenting a controversial work at the Ontario Art Gallery. In *La petite danse sans nom* (1980) the dancer-choreographer paced the stage dressed in a peasant dress carrying a pail. After a long silence, she squatted to urinate in the pot, and then exited. The act brought her overnight notoriety. An excursion into conceptual artmaking, the piece showed dance to be a medium for mastery of the body, where not only the mind is a muscle, but the bladder is one, too. Reviewing the Montreal premiere of the work in *Le Devoir*, Angèle Dagenais wrote: "In Toronto, Marie Chouinard scandalized her audience by transforming the stage into a rest room. In Montreal, the public smiled at her naive and provocative candor without insisting on it. With her pretty face and body, it was easy to smile at her 'tantrums.'"[1] These remarks underscore not only the difference in social attitudes between audiences in Montreal and Ontario, but also the persistence of distinct cultural sensibilities in French and English Canada.

Another performance "action" devised by Chouinard took place at Café Campus in 1981. *Danseuse cherche amoureux ou amoureuse pour la nuit du 1er juin*, or "Woman Dancer Seeks Male or Female Lover for the Night of June 1," was a "love call" that demanded the participation of the audience. Blindfolded, Chouinard twirled in place, a flashlight in her hands. When she became dizzy, she stopped: the person upon whom the beam of the flashlight fell was thus chosen to be her partner for the night. The rules of the game encroached on those of real life. Here, again, was a work where art and reality were willfully confused, in this case, in a staged version of "spin the bottle."

Unlike Margie Gillis, who also produces one-woman shows, Chouinard thrives on provocation, although her work lacks the accusatory tone of Fortier's. In fact,

Marie Chouinard in *STAB (Space Time and Beyond)*.
Photograph by Louise Oligny.

Chouinard can be seen as a modern primitive who bares her private world, even when this entails the enactment of intimate actions such as urinating and masturbating. Although her performances turn on the flesh, they seem closer to an initiation into sensual pleasure. The awakening of the senses appears in simple images: washing her long blond hair, munching an apple or a green pepper, or smearing herself with mud—actions that appear, respectively, in *Marie chien noir* (1982), *Mimas lune de Saturne* (1980), and *Crue* (1981).

Chouinard finds inspiration in sources as varied as Japanese butoh, visual installations, performance art, and African dancing. She incorporates text, voice, sound, body language, and eroticism in an iconoclastic style that naturally has its quota of shock elements. In *STAB (Space Time and Beyond)* (1987), she wore a G-string and metal cothurni, while her body was painted blood red. A disproportionately long antenna, suggesting a horn of plenty, served as her headdress. Guttural sounds accompanied gestures invoking centaurs, minotaurs, unicorns, the Greek god Pan, primitive warriors, and a host of other mythic creatures.

STAB was a preliminary study, a prelude to her *L'Après-midi d'un faune*, also created in 1987. Inspired by photographs of Vaslav Nijinsky, who not also danced the title role but also choreographed the first, controversial production of this work, Chouinard offered a rereading of his *succès de scandale* that showed a concern for history, although viewed through the lens of postmodernism. Faithful to Nijinsky's profile

Marie Chinouard in *L'Après-midi d'un faune*.

stance, she likewise retained his use of lateral movement evoking the two-dimensional style of ancient friezes.

Chouinard also brought an androgynous and contemporary dimension to the work, thus updating the controversy around its sexual theme and autoeroticism. The nymphs who figure in Nijinsky's version are replaced by shafts of incandescent light that Chouinard, in the role of the Faun, endeavors again and again to penetrate. The languor of Nijinsky's opening recumbent pose is replaced by the image of a standing amazon with goat horns on her head. Padding one of her thighs and the opposite calf to recall Nijinsky's powerful musculature, Chouinard wore a single clog—a fitting counterpoint to the single breast possessed by the amazons. Numerous small needles jutted through the fabric covering her right shoulder and breast, as well as her left thigh. The sexual and drug connotations were definitely contemporary.

Breaking one of the horns, she placed it like a phallus over her sex evoking a satyr of antiquity. She then sheathed it with a red condom, a gesture that telescoped the sexuality of the 1980s and the ever-present anguish of AIDS. The needles pricked her flesh, recalling the injections of a heroin addict in search of new sensations and instant pleasures. Like an animal in heat, she offered her last spasm—without Nijinsky's scarf—while the shaft of light in which she lies prostrate "ejaculated" a shower of silver sequins.

Although thoroughly postmodern, the iconography of *STAB* and *Faune* is as controversial as that of Nijinsky's prototype at the time of its creation in 1912. Chouinard refracts rather than reflects her source, taking poetic license with the original in a rereading that adds to the meanings of the work accumulated over time.

The intimate acts of Chouinard's iconoclastic and sensual world are performed with a combination of audacity and candor, placing the audience in the passive role of a voyeur. Whereas other iconoclasts of the Montreal scene have had to wait years for recognition and notoriety, the sensationalism and seductiveness of Chouinard's works have rapidly propelled her to the Canadian and international spotlight. Clearly, the public is more receptive to provocation when this comes with the allure of primitivism.

In her most recent pieces, Chouinard has tackled group choreography for the first time. *Les Trous du ciel* (1991) draws inspiration from Eskimo culture, although the work retains her characteristic primitivism. *Le Sacre du Printemps* (1993), set to the Stravinsky score to which Nijinsky had created a primitivist choreography even more controversial than *Faune*, is Chouinard's vision of the explosiveness of primal life at the moment of birth.

Howard Richard

Montrealer Howard Richard came to choreography by way of classical ballet. His attentiveness to gestural detail and choreographic craft sets him apart from other dancemakers working in his native city.

Richard gave his first full-length concert in 1985. Before that time, he had danced, taught, and on occasion choreographed for Eddy Toussaint's company and for Pointépiénu. Trained in classical, modern, and tap dancing, all of which have left an imprint on his work, Richard has been deeply influenced by Twyla Tharp, one of his stylistic models. Like her, he mixes different styles in works that are carefully thought out and polished, even though the final product is deliberately accessible rather than intellectual. Typically, his dances are crafted during a long rehearsal period.

Richard's music—classical, hard rock, new age—is as varied as his sources. His dance language is highly individual and sets him apart from the proponents of Montreal dance theater. Younger than Fortier and Perreault, he regards himself as belonging to another choreographic generation: indeed, his company, Howard Richard Danse, is a comparatively recent phenomenon. He has a nucleus of full-time dancers, while other dancers, members of Les Ballets Jazz de Montréal, Les Grands Ballets Canadiens, Fortier Danse Création, and other Montreal troupes, perform with his company on an occasional basis, depending upon their schedules.

It is because his works bring together a number of choreographic tendencies that professionals are attracted to him. Neither a purist nor a social radical, Richard has developed his own demanding aesthetic based on complex rhythms and intricate movements that can only be performed by dancers with solid technical training. By focusing on the basic compositional elements of a dance—time, space, energy—he toys with order and chaos in each of his works. Unlike other French Canadian choreographers, he does not emphasize design in his productions, possibly for financial reasons. Instead, he concentrates on the choreographic elements of a work and on pushing even further an imagination rich in movement and rhythmic resources. In addition to refining his craft from piece to piece, he has gradually expanded his emotional register, seeking to infuse his work with feeling—something that few of his contemporaries are willing to do.

Marc Lalonde and Kathie Renaud in Howard Richard's *Les Baigneurs.*
Photograph by Robert Laliberté.

Richard creates accessible, moving works. *La Femme aux talons hauts* (1985), also known as *Woman With High Heels*, is a provocative solo, performed by a woman who spends the entire piece dancing—and exposing her vulnerability—to a man who sits smoking a cigarette with his back to the audience. Taken into the repertory of Les Ballets Jazz de Montréal, the work was performed on the company's world tours. Richard attends to every detail of his choreographic cameos, often giving them titles evocative of paintings—*Woman Reclining on a Chair* (1986), for instance, or *Les Baigneurs* (or *The Bathers*, 1987), an athletic duet set in the Roaring Twenties, or even *Colors* (1988), an Apollonian work. Another piece, *Several Stories* (1986), to music by Sergei Rachmaninoff, takes place at a cocktail party. Various social situations unfold around a sofa in this happy-hour mood piece, by turns brilliant and subtle.

Richard's finest work, however, is *Dissonance* (1988), which speaks to the difficulty of male-female relationships. Isolated in their respective pools of light, a man and a woman dialogue by gestures, or rather they deliver simultaneous monologues. The piece builds in emotional intensity, ending in a powerful rape scene to Franz Schubert's *Ave Maria* that in its play of contrasts strikes the ultimate chord of dissonance.

Richard's choreographic sensibility occupies a special place in Montreal's dance fresco. Like Montanaro, he has evolved outside the mainstream of the avant-garde. He presents intimate portraits or group pieces with a more dramatic theme. Among the latter are *Borderline* (1986), exposing the misdeeds of war, and *Italian Suite* (1985), a danced melodrama. Although he is not a proponent of Montreal's brand of New Dance, Richard has succeeded in creating a public for his work. Less well known than Montanaro or Chouinard, he is not yet in a position to tour internationally and must still work on a small scale. His talent is obvious, and given favorable circumstances and enhanced resources, he will almost certainly find the broad market that his work deserves.

IX

Cultural Ambassadors and Popularizers

Two opposing schools of thought prevail in Montreal's dance community. The first—and dominant—one gives highest priority to creation and innovation; the second, more traditional, works against the tide, intent on making dance more popular. A portrait of professional dance in Montreal would be incomplete were it limited only to the city's creative innovators, ignoring the many who have served, and continue to serve, as cultural ambassadors, acquainting the public-at-large with an art outside the "elitist" mold.

Although such initiatives tend to be less innovative, their importance cannot be underestimated. To deny their presence on the Montreal scene would be tantamount to denying the existence of the men and women who have labored to popularize dance by challenging its hermetic image. In so doing, they have paved the way to an acceptance of the more radical and engaged approaches of many Québécois choreographers. By making dance more accessible, these "popularizers" have won over a new public, offering it, moreover, a basic frame of reference. The dance landscape of Montreal would be very different were it not for their efforts.

Entre-Six, or Ballet on a Shoestring

A student of Gérald Crevier, Séda Zaré, and Elizabeth Lesse, Jacqueline Lemieux-Lopez (1939-1979) was struck by cancer while still in her twenties. A successful operation gave her a twelve-year reprieve. Living now on borrowed time, she dedicated the rest of her life to promoting dance both in her native Quebec and in Canada generally, with the aim of enhancing its respectability and broadening its audience.

Donning many hats throughout her career, Lemieux-Lopez was first and foremost a remarkable teacher of ballet. She served as Ludmilla Chiriaeff's assistant at the Ecole Supérieure de Danse du Québec and at the academy affiliated with Les Grands Ballets Canadiens, in addition to heading the Académie de Ballet du Saguenay in the Lac Saint-Jean area of Quebec. She was also the cofounder and administrator of the chamber ballet company Entre-Six. To all these undertakings she brought dedication, generosity, and a spirit of entrepreneurship, as well as a high degree of efficiency that reflected her sense of urgency. Time was running out on her.

Her initial efforts were devoted to exploring new methods of classical training. Traveling to Europe and the United States, she worked with master teachers, retaining from each the technical and anatomical insights that she would apply in her own teaching. She subsequently opened professional training centers throughout the province of Quebec. Québec Eté Danse, a summer program inaugurated in 1976, survived her death by some years. Located in Lennoxville on the campus of Bishop's University, the

Jacqueline Lemieux-Lopez teaching at L'Ecole Supérieure de Danse du Québec.

program was modeled, albeit on a smaller scale, on the American Dance Festival and
Jacob's Pillow, and intended as a dance counterpart to existing music camps. An international roster of teachers gave intensive courses in ballet, modern dance, jazz, and
creative dance. A refresher course for teachers was also offered. Meanwhile, evening
performances brought students in direct contact with North American professional
companies and Canadian stars such as Karen Kain and Frank Augustyn.

Lemieux-Lopez then assumed the direction of the Académie de Ballet du Saguenay
in an effort to decentralize professional training, which was concentrated in Montreal.
The instruction was solid, based on the RAD and Cecchetti methods, while also including work in modern dance and jazz. In response to the parochialism of the Québécois
dance world, she organized the 1978 Octobre en Danse Festival, which featured dance
artists from all over Canada. During the festival, the Quebec public discovered Margie
Gillis (then at the start of her career) and Judith Marcuse, both Montrealers, and redis-
covered Françoise Sullivan and Françoise Riopelle, two pioneers of Montreal dance.

At that time, Lemieux-Lopez was also teaching company class at Les Grands Ballets Canadiens. There she met Lawrence Gradus, a soloist with the company who was
also a choreographer. The encounter marked the beginning of a long personal and professional partnership. Together, in 1976, they created Entre-Six, a minitroupe of six
dancers, all from Quebec. Following the tradition of Les Compagnons de la Danse, the
chamber company founded by Ludmilla Chiriaeff that had folded some years before for

lack of funding, Entre-Six toured schools, colleges, and universities, while also appearing in "pocket" theaters. With a repertory largely choreographed by Gradus, the company wanted to make ballet accessible.

Born in New York, Gradus had danced for American Ballet Theatre, Jerome Robbins's Ballets: U.S.A., and the Louisville Ballet before joining Les Grands Ballets Canadiens. His work for Entre-Six was inspired by the choreographic language of Antony Tudor, but without the psychological aspect so typical of the latter's works. Most of Gradus's ballets were abstract works, and from the start the company toured them throughout Canada, the United States, and Europe. (These tours amounted to some 100 performances a year.) In *Emergence*, Gradus made one of his few incursions into dance theater, although the ballet's intimate drama unfolds without a definite story line. *Nonetto*, by contrast, revealed the Apollonian lyricism and sustained musicality that were his strong points as a choreographer. In *Toccata*, he deftly crafted a light, acrobatic pas de quatre, while in *En Mouvement* he created an abstract sketch to an electronic score commissioned from Vincent Dionne. The company also initiated a series of children's ballets, which brought out the choreographer's humor and fondness

Entre-Six: Jacques Drapeau, Shelley Osher, and Christine Clair in Lawrence Gradus's *Queen's Variations*.

for the unexpected. *Peter and the Wolf* and *Des Eléphants et...* were the best of these innovative efforts.

The company's reputation quickly spread beyond Quebec. Easy to tour, and with an unpretentious repertory that catered to a broad public, the troupe performed all over Canada. As administrator, Lemieux-Lopez skillfully navigated among government funding agencies. Highly respected within the dance community, she was asked to serve on the board of the Dance in Canada Association and as a consultant for the Canada Council, which, after her death, created an annual prize in her name. An enlightened missionary for her art, she organized a dance symposium in 1977 and wrote a paper in response to the proposals laid out by Minister of Culture Jean-Paul L'Allier in the government document known as "Le Livre Vert." In her response, she insisted upon the need for broad professional training in dance, training that would include modern dance as well as ballet, along with various creative approaches.

In 1979, cancer struck again, this time with no possibility of remission. When death came, Entre-Six was at the point of financial collapse. Early in 1980, the troupe folded, leaving a vacuum that has yet to be filled in Montreal. In its half-dozen years of existence, Entre-Six had offered healthy competition to Les Grands Ballets Canadiens, while instilling an appreciation of ballet among younger audiences. After the death of his wife and the disbanding of their company, Gradus left for Ottawa, where he founded the Theatre Ballet of Canada, eventually renamed the Ottawa Ballet, in an attempt to revive the spirit of Entre-Six in the Canadian capital.

The Margie Gillis Cult

A Montreal dancer of great expressive range, Margie Gillis is among the figures best known to the general public. She was born into a family of outstanding athletes: her parents Gene Gillis and Rhona Wurtele are former Olympic ski champions; her brother Jere played hockey for the Vancouver Canucks, while her other brother, the late Christopher Gillis, danced with the companies of José Limón and Paul Taylor. Margie, who took her first ballet class at the age of three, would also bring honor on the family, becoming the object of a cult that now extends far beyond the dance community.

She first came to public attention in 1976, when she worked with Linda Rabin on the project that became *The White Goddess*. Encouraged by this remarkable experience and the popularity that followed from her appearance in the work, Gillis went off to New York to study for a year. On her return to Montreal, she gave a solo concert of her work at a matinee sponsored by the Octobre en Danse Festival. With this, the Montreal public discovered her astonishing range of expression. Thanks to her charisma and the emotion that spilled so generously from her presence, she quickly became an audience favorite.

Since then, Gillis has usually performed to sold-out houses. She brings an immediacy to the universal themes personalized in her dances, which are generally set to popular music. Gillis's work lies outside Montreal's new dance movement, although she shares with its vanguard choreographers a highly individualistic approach. Her stage personae are refinements of lived experience. At once intimate and universal, her creations invite an acceptance of dance in general, while displaying an expressive range that transcends the conventions of the classical. Situated midway between the linear abstraction associated with ballet and the social commitment of avant-garde work, her dances bridge the extremes represented by the two forms. From the start, Gillis toured

ABOVE: Margie Gillis giving a lecture-demonstration in Beijing. Photograph by Jack Udashkin.

RIGHT: Margie Gillis and Christopher Gillis in Paul Taylor's *Duet*. Photograph by Michael Slobodian.

extensively, first on the Quebec college circuit, then nationally across Canada, and, finally, internationally, all the while building her reputation.

In 1979, Gillis followed the old silk route to China. While visiting the gardens of Beijing, she started dancing to some music on her cassette recorder. A fascinated crowd immediately surrounded her. As a result of this impromptu recital, she was invited to dance at the Beijing Opera House and to give lecture-demonstrations on modern dance a few days later. The Chinese were astonished by her way of moving: at the time, Western modern dance was completely unknown in China. Thus, she became an ambassador for her country as well as an ambassador for her art. Gillis made numerous world tours, visiting the Far East, New Zealand, and the South Pacific. Everywhere she went, her spontaneity and charisma led people to compare her to Isadora Duncan, to speak of her, even, as Duncan's reincarnation.

Indeed, audiences easily identify with Gillis's dances, which are expressive, fluid, and free in form, and with the Pre- Raphaelite beauty of her face and Lady Godiva mane. Her place within the panorama of Montreal dance is analogous to that occupied during the 1970s by cult figures like Janis Joplin or Joan Baez. She speaks out, as they did, for human rights and often dances for free at fundraising benefits for organizations such as Amnesty International and Global Disarmament. Moreover, she performs her one-woman shows with the intensity that both Joplin and Baez brought to the stage, drawing power exclusively from lived experience, as though she were forever dancing her life and living her dance. Like a naive painter, she reveals a great simplicity and a great sensibility, qualities that appeal to her audience, especially the young generation of dancegoers for whom she has become a role model.

Although Gillis prefers to dance her own works, she has at times collaborated with other choreographers and companies. In both cases, she makes the role her own, giving it the personal touch and emotional intensity that set her apart from other Montreal dancers. Widely acclaimed as a cultural ambassador of Canada both for efforts to popularize dance and her many world tours, she received the Order of Canada while still in her early thirties.

The Craze for Jazz Ballet

The creation of Les Ballets Jazz de Montréal in 1972 gave legitimacy to an extremely popular current in Quebec dance. The craze for jazz ballet swept the province like a tidal wave in the 1970s. Although the initial enthusiasm has abated, Les Ballets Jazz remains the most traveled company of Quebec, perhaps even of the entire country.

Extremely popular in big cities, the company has made numerous world tours, including Latin America, Africa, and the Far East. The repertory does not particularly reflect a Québécois sensibility. On the contrary, it draws much of its inspiration from American sources. Yet the hybrid mixture of classical and jazz style dancing remains peculiar to Quebec.

Born in Séda Zaré's basement studio, Les Ballets Jazz was the brainchild of Eva von Gencsy, a former ballerina of the Royal Winnipeg Ballet and Les Grands Ballets Canadiens as well as the creator of the Montreal style of jazz ballet, and her student, the Haitian-born Eddy Toussaint. The two became the artistic directors of the new ensemble, with Geneviève Salbaing joining the team as company administrator. Toussaint's association with Les Ballets Jazz was short-lived: within a year misunderstandings and quarrels over financial matters would lead him to form a company of his own.

Les Ballets Jazz Contemporains: Eva von Gencsy (left), Lee Gagnon, Eddy Toussaint, Geneviève Salbaing, and Marcel Dubé at a production meeting for Gencsy's *Jeremie*, 1973.

Initially, Les Ballets Jazz was a showcase for the hybrid style developed and popularized by von Gencsy through her work for television. Indeed, the original troupe had been a merger of Toussaint's student dance group, Rétros, and von Gencsy's professional television dancers.

Although Les Ballets Jazz was formed to promote jazz ballet, it was initially named Les Ballets Jazz Contemporains. This catchall title was later replaced by Les Ballets Jazz de Montréal, chiefly to identify the group on its many international tours. With her charisma and enormous popularity, von Gencsy was the company's spearhead. However, she, too, eventually abandoned ship, preferring to pursue her career as a master teacher giving clinics around the world, and the artistic direction was assumed by Salbaing, the company's former administrator.

Despite its enormous popularity, Les Ballets Jazz faced many difficulties. The Canada Council refused to subsidize the company (although project grants were occasionally awarded), since operating grants could only be used to support ballet or experimental groups: jazz ballet fell into neither category. Some Council members took the view that the company's work was commercial rather than innovative and thus undeserving of federal subsidy. Although, generally, this attitude still persists, the Council has somewhat modified its policy, and the company is now funded.

Despite additional support from municipal and provincial funding agencies, the bulk of the company's budget continues to come from touring and private fundraising. Les Ballets Jazz is among the very few companies to employ its dancers on a year-round basis (rather than laying them off periodically to cut costs). Another source of income, until recently at least, has been the company's network of affiliated schools. However, with the end of the dance boom and the waning popularity of jazz ballet, these schools have all closed down.

From the start, the problem of funding was tied up with the difficulty of identifying the company's style. Although jazz ballet was a Quebec invention, jazz itself was an American form. Why, then, should Canadians fund it? Moreover, with its classical steps, hip thrusts, and "sexy" performance style, jazz ballet was viewed as being closer to Broadway than to art, or at least to what the Montreal dance community regarded as art, even if the Quebec form did not display the glamorous trappings of the Broadway stage. Another point of contention was the movement language: it was not "Québécois." Yet another criticism concerned the sets and costumes, which were kept to a bare minimum, no doubt because the company's heavy touring schedule precluded the use of elaborate decors and stage effects. Finally, the company was taken to task for having too few Canadian dancers, a phenomenon linked to its "commercial" image and endless touring, which encouraged rapid turnover among the dancers.

Yet for the public-at-large jazz ballet amounted to a veritable craze. Unlike ballet, it had no elitist aura, nor did it offer the intellectual and hermetic approach of contemporary dance. Instead, it satisfied the thirst for physical expression so pervasive in the 1960s and 1970s, a thirst revealed in the cult of the body and sexuality, the fad for fit-

Les Ballets Jazz de Montréal: Hans Vancol and Odette Lalonde in Ulysses Dove's *Bad Blood*, 1984. Photograph by Ian Westbury.

ness, jogging, exercise, and aerobics. Along with students and professional dancers, ordinary fans flocked to take classes with members of Les Ballets Jazz whenever the company came to town.

Beginning in the 1980s, the modern dance style associated with the American choreographer Louis Falco began to replace the vogue for jazz ballet. Wisely, Les Ballet Jazz included one of Falco's works, *Escargot*, in its repertory. Falco updated the lyricism of Humphrey-Limón technique, infusing it with an energy that was both eye-catching and sensational. Technical virtuosity was pushed to the limits: indeed, it became the very premise of his movement style. The Montreal public was conquered, and both Falco and his New York associate Jennifer Muller quickly attracted a following within the local dance community. A typical Falco warm-up included the physical and aerobic exercises of jazz ballet, but done in a way that was closer to modern dance. Traces of his style can be found in Ginette Laurin's high-energy idiom and even in the work of Edouard Lock, especially his way of performing speeded-up movement with both virtuosity and casualness.

The Falco fad acted as a transition: jazz ballet now moved increasingly in the direction of contemporary dance. Young choreographers, in turn, assimilated elements of the technique, which they viewed as a dynamic alternative to the period's reigning minimalism. This thirst for "physicality," which overlapped with the fashion for breakdancing, was a widespread phenomenon in the early 1980s.

Jazz ballet had offered a popular alternative to ballet and modern dance. With time, however, its appeal diminished even among its erstwhile public. Sports complexes and fitness centers began to offer aerobics classes, thus competing with Les Ballets Jazz's own schools. Enrollments dwindled, and, eventually, the schools were closed, including the company's "feeder" academy in Montreal. Meanwhile, Canadian choreographers were contributing fewer and fewer works to the company's repertory.

Today, the company's artistic vision is less clear than at any previous time. Some works in the repertory are openly contemporary in style, while others are decidedly classical, even being danced on pointe. Moreover, the music retains few links with jazz, initially the company's inspiration. Instead, the strength of the company lies in its solid international reputation and instinct for survival, this, despite the slippery ground over which it now skates. Fifteen years ago, Les Ballets Jazz held an enviable place in the Quebec dance community. Diligent management, team spirit, and decent pay for the dancers brought it stability. Salbaing's recent retirement closed an important chapter in the company's history. She was replaced by William Whitener, an American with a modern dance background and experience on Broadway. Whitener, however, left the company in 1994 to become artistic director of the Royal Winnipeg Ballet. Les Ballets Jazz is now headed by Mauricio Wainrot, a South American choreographer based in Montreal.

Eddy Toussaint and the Star System

Within a year of his abrupt departure from Les Ballets Jazz, Eddy Toussaint had founded his own company along with an affiliated school. The goal of Compagnie Eddy Toussaint was to popularize the art of dance in Quebec. To do this, Toussaint created works to music by popular Quebec bands. Although the company fell into the category of neither jazz nor contemporary dance, it was a long way from the neoclassicism that would later characterize it.

From year to year the company gained ground with the general public. Toussaint's works showed a concern for line and acrobatic partnering. Often abstract and performed without decor, they were typically danced to well-known popular music. At the start of its fifth season, however, the company did a sudden about-face: its work turned increasingly classical. Soft slippers gave way to pointe shoes; hip thrusts to arabesques. The metamorphosis was made possible by five years of intensive classical training under the watchful eye of Camila Malashenko, an exponent of Russian teaching methods. With this shift, the company ceased to present itself as a contemporary ensemble, billing itself instead as a neoclassical one.

The Toussaint "formula" differed from that of Montreal's senior ballet institution in a number of respects. Les Grands Ballets Canadiens did not produce international stars. Toussaint, on the other, cultivated the star system from the start. His talent, however, was home-grown, trained, in most cases, at his own school. One such graduate

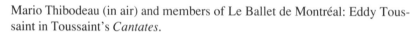

Mario Thibodeau (in air) and members of Le Ballet de Montréal: Eddy Toussaint in Toussaint's *Cantates*.

Le Ballet de Montréal: Eddy Toussaint: Sophie Bissonnette, Louis Robitaille,
and Denis Dulude in Toussaint's *Souvenance*. Photograph by Melodie Garbish.

was Louis Robitaille, a Toussaint star who spent a season with Les Grands Ballets
Canadiens as a guest artist. On occasion, too, he danced with European ballet companies, as did Anik Bissonnette, his partner and future wife, who had also trained at the
Toussaint school. Acclaimed by critics and audiences alike, the couple became the
object of a personality cult, a cult that Toussaint—with the help of the media—actively
encouraged. International recognition came in 1984 with the couple's prize-winning
performance at the International Ballet Competition in Helsinki. Mario Thibodeau,
Denis Dulude, Jean-Marc Lebeau, and Sophie Bissonnette (Anik's twin sister) were
other company stars who developed a local following and also danced abroad as guest
artists.

Toussaint's vision of popularizing classical dancing and creating stars did not work
to the company's advantage, at least in terms of the dance community and the Canada
Council. Although both the provincial government and the city of Montreal supported
the company financially, federal agencies consistently turned down its applications for
funding. Thus, to stave off the ever-present threat of extinction, the company had to
seek private corporate funding. In an effort to garner business support, the company
changed its name in 1985 to Le Ballet de Montréal: Eddy Toussaint. The strategy
proved unsuccessful. However, a new modus operandi soon presented itself: Le Ballet
de Montréal was invited by the state of Florida for a three-month residency—all
expenses paid. As a harbinger of "free trade" on the North American continent, the ini-
tiative was full of promise.

International exposure was not limited to this side of the Atlantic. Le Ballet de Montréal stars appeared with the Odessa Ballet in *Swan Lake*, while principals from Odessa joined the Montreal company in 1988 for a series of performances at the Place des Arts. Moreover, works by Toussaint entered the repertory of companies in France as well as the United States.

For all his fame, Toussaint remained controversial both as an artist and public personality. His repertory was eclectic, and the flashiness of many works invited critical attack as much as praise. The technical mastery of the dancers trained at his school was never in question, however. Toussaint's choreography catered to a general audience that did not seek invention in dance but was satisfied by technical prowess. If *Dam Ballah* (1976) explored his Haitian roots, *Façades* (1982) succumbed to the tango vogue, while *Cantates* (1978), a dance for men wearing long circular skirts, emulated Béjart. In his effort to demystify dance, Toussaint also choreographed works based on French Canadian legends, including *Alexis le Trotteur* (1978) and a version of *Rose LaTulippe* (1979). As for his signature piece, *Un Simple Moment* (1980), this easily became a vehicle displaying the technique and expressive qualities of the Robitaille-Bissonnette duo. But it was only with *New World Symphony* (1986), created during his second Florida residency and later performed in Montreal, that Toussaint showed significant development as a choreographer. In this ballet, he refined his means, while highlighting the physical power and technique of his dancers, most of whom were trained at his school.

In the beginning, Toussaint's main interest was making ballet accessible to the general public. Gradually, his ambitions changed. Dissatisfied with the company's neoclassical image and determined to challenge persistent criticism of his work as being shallow in content, he now became thoroughly classical. With his zany, updated version of *The Nutcracker*, created in 1987, he showed that he was ready to tackle the classics.

This shift in goal raised some basic questions. Did Montreal need a second classical company to compete with Les Grands Ballets Canadiens? Was Canada prepared to subsidize a fourth large-scale classical company? In a province like Quebec, where theatrical dance was openly geared to innovation, Toussaint's sudden return to the conventions of old-fashioned classicism went against the grain of the entire development of dance since the 1960s.

In the late 1980s, the company was shaken by a number of dramatic events. Saddled with debts, badly managed, and on the brink of bankruptcy, the company was unable to pay its dancers, who nevertheless continued to perform without salary for six months. Eventually, the payless paydays took their toll, and the company's ranks emptied. The greatest blow came when Anik Bissonnette and Louis Robitaille left to join Les Grands Ballets Canadiens. Without the trump card of his stars, Toussaint could do little to keep the company from folding. In February 1990, after a low-key press conference, Le Ballet de Montréal: Eddy Toussaint formally disbanded.

For its part, the management of Les Grands Ballets Canadiens has made full use of Toussaint's former stars after a trial period during which few challenging roles came their way. Once this period was over, they received their customary billing. At the same time, the company began to promote its other principals as stars through strategically placed articles publicizing the dancers' personal and professional lives. In so doing, Les Grands Ballets Canadiens has finally adopted the policy of the National Ballet of Canada and the Royal Winnipeg Ballet, which have capitalized for decades on a roster of homegrown superstars.

X

Postscript:
At the Dawn of a New Millennium

*In short, caught between collective psychotherapy and an Anglophone dance
elite, French Canadians no longer know where to turn. One also wonders
whether the aristocratic ballet reflects their aspirations. Russian ballet is a
legacy of the tsars; the Paris Opéra caters to a financial elite—as do all of
Europe's ballet shrines, where the intervals, as the partisans of modern
dance are wont to say, are as much an attraction for the perfumed and
bejeweled crowd as the performances themselves. Religion alone did not
keep the pupils of Madame Chiriaeff from striking a regal pose. True, one
must study the basics of classical dance to acquire a solid technique. But,
then, it should be possible to leave it and do something worthwhile. We shall
doubtless never succeed in inventing a Québécois dance, as some school and
company leaflets foolishly promise, knowing that there is no such thing as
Russian, or Belgian, or French dance, only individual choreographers and,
occasionally, national traditions. In time it would be nice for us to establish
a tradition crossing the last of the stumbling blocks that derive from within.¹*

The Wave of the Future

Over the years, professional dance in Quebec has endured, even if its course has been
far from smooth. Happily, dance is no longer an object of religious persecution and
social prejudice. Yet, it remains, even today, widely misunderstood by the public-at-
large, albeit to a lesser degree than formerly.

No longer under the wing of the church, Montreal theatrical dance has finally
received its due in terms of recognition, not only at the national level, but also internationally. To say, however, that it has fully established itself would be to err on the side
of optimism. Still, dance in Quebec has given proof of an amazing tenacity as well as
an amazing diversity, reflected in works that can be intimate in nature or politically
engaged, culturally specific or purely abstract. What lies ahead?

As we near the year 2000, the pendulum of history is swinging, paradoxically,
toward a retrieval of the past, albeit a past that has been transformed. After an era spent
searching for identity and conquering cultural territory, the Quebec art world is being
swept by winds of change. The times are marked by cultural uncertainty and fatigue.
Among the new stakes are free trade, the failure of the Canadian electorate to ratify the
Meech Lake Accord (which was to recognize Quebec as "a distinct society" and grant
it independent political status within Canada), and the changing demographics of the
province's ethnic makeup. These factors call into question the very essence of Québécois identity and the role of the artist in Québécois society.

119

Quebec's possible secession from Canada and the ratification of the North American Free Trade Agreement raise new issues that must be addressed. Is Québécois culture and, by extension, Québécois choreographic culture, a heritage to be overprotected or should it be opened to influences originating elsewhere? In the face of this dilemma and in view of the increasing globalization of cultural space, Québécois artists have chosen to look outward rather than inward. Like artists elsewhere, they embrace the notion of "transculturalism" in all its multiethnic dimensions, along with the idea of moving across and between disciplines.

The history of dance in Montreal is chiefly one of revolutions, as opposed to evolutions, with dances prematurely born, raw and unfinished, their process of development still incomplete. It is a history, too, that branches out, forming clusters and fragmenting into numerous individual and independent trajectories. If the absence of models has often favored creativity, it has, at times, also engendered creative islands and closed communities, deliberately shielded from external influences by cultural amnesia.

For many, this is the time to retrieve, however indirectly, the fragments of a history that is now being courted. There is a replay in a minor key of ideas from the past; this time, however, the ideas are deconstructed, taken out of context, seemingly suspended in a void. A plurality of currents appears, and in Quebec, as elsewhere, hybridization is the password. Edouard Lock's intentional borrowings from Indian music and the technical vocabulary of classical dance in *New Demons* are an example of this stylistic crossbreeding, as is his alliance of a "heavy metal" sensibility with the virtuosity of ballet.

Images, choreographic or otherwise, are piled up, creating a whole that is not one and whose guiding principle is "impurity," in the sense of the term as used by Guy Scarpeta.[2] Composite images, rather than dream icons, stream before us. Works are overcoded, with multiple layers of meaning—thickets of choreographic discourse that only the lucky can penetrate. Interpretative possibilities and avenues of exploration are innumerable. High tech is present in Michael Montanaro's work, but absent from the choreography of Daniel Léveillé and Jean-Pierre Perreault, who approach the act of creation through architectural design.

If the fear of associating with the past seems to have ended, along with the need to cast off the entire burden of tradition, there is still no obvious desire for permanence. Continuity implies a school, where the artistic torch, representing the codified visions of the past, is passed from old to young, the generation of the future. In Montreal, this does not occur, at least among experimental dancemakers. Today's choreographers display no sense of history and make no allusion to a collective memory. They retrieve fragments of the past casually and eccentrically, and persist in working independently, isolated from any larger context. No school for training future dancers is affiliated with today's experimental companies, thus ensuring their own impermanence. Yet, these same companies and choreographers insist upon dancers who are versatile and technically skilled.

Certain overall trends can be discerned however. An ecological mood pervades Montreal, that Paul-André Fortier has captured better than most. *Le Mythe décisif* deals with the destruction of the natural environment for venal ends. *Désert* roundly condemns a consumer society imprisoned in industrial debris, indifferent to the recycling of its own wastes. These works go beyond the social and political engagement of the choreographer's earlier works by addressing universal contemporary concerns.

Stylistically, there is a return to minimalism. In many works the choreographic content is almost nonexistent, pushed to the limits of nondance. Léveillé's *Mémoires d'un temps ravagé* offers three snapshot images in forty-five minutes. Even though the images themselves are visually arresting, they exist in a deliberate gestural vacuum. With its contemplative atmosphere akin to Zen, *Mémoires* offers a gallery of choreographic still lifes. *A force d'y penser, on y pense de moins en moins (Thinking so much of it I manage to forget it)*, created by Léveillé in 1989, adopts a similar approach. Perreault's experiments of the past eight years follow much the same pattern. With their multiple variations on a single theme, his cyclical projects are built upon materials that he continually reworks, making abundant use of self-reference.

The gestural frenzy of Lock's work or Ginette Laurin's is diametrically opposed to such minimalism. Resolutely North American, their sensibility belongs to a world of fast food, video clips, and breakdancing.

Future Prospects

In the face of such contradictions and given the nonhierarchical cohabitation of cultural and stylistic borrowings, the historian can only take the moment's pulse. The need to personalize discourse is always present. If romanticism was born of the fear of becoming homogenized, then, today, we are experiencing a return to romanticism. In this neoromanticism, the individual is triumphant and all creative scenarios allowed, while symbolism resurfaces along with figurative art.

In sketching the landscape of Montreal dance in the near future, one should note an improvement in the system of artistic support. With private enterprise now taking a more favorable view of the culture industry, dance has drawn closer to the business world in marketing and day-to-day management. Recession has taken its toll, however, and the public monies allocated to the arts will almost certainly diminish. Government agencies are aware that frittering away funds in subsidies to small companies and independent choreographers improves neither the condition of dance nor its public image: the profession continues to be regarded as marginal. Thus, the creation of the Agora de la Danse, a theater exclusively devoted to dance, is extremely significant. Heavily subsidized by the Ministry of Cultural Affairs of Quebec and the Université du Québec à Montréal (UQAM), the Agora de la Danse offers independent choreographers a venue for experiment and performance throughout the year. The space exists, but whether a high degree of creativity can be sustained in the long term remains an open question. Signs of exhaustion have already appeared in the present generation of dancemakers.

Reared in better conditions than their elders, today's young choreographers have proved to be greedier. They have higher expectations and are unwilling to remain gypsies in Montreal's bohemian world. Will they shake off the burden of continuous innovation and distinguish themselves from the previous generation? Only time will tell.

Is Montreal dance an alternative culture, a popular culture, or an elite one? The audience that exists for jazz and ballet is completely different from the audience existing for experimental dance. The first is an establishment public of business people and members of the bourgeoisie who buy season tickets for the offerings at the Place des Arts. New dance, by contrast, attracts the intelligentsia, students, and artists of the avant-garde. The public-at-large, however, remains as illiterate about dance as ever—despite the recent boom. For this public, dance is embarrassing and intimidating, incomprehensible and exotic.

As a cultural metropolis, Montreal is host to several international art festivals. If the city has become a citizen of the world cultural polity, dance has yet to attain full legitimacy in this enlarged context. Moreover, Montreal dance still fails to offer a spectrum of styles that is genuinely broad and popular. Within the dance community itself, artists often shun one another, taking refuge in cliques and cultivating their preferred genres, save for a few isolated and unfruitful attempts to unite ballet and experimental dance.

As lost as one may feel in the forest of Quebec dance, one can also glimpse on the horizon an end to the trees. Only when a cultural strategy embracing dance in all its myriad forms comes into being will the game temporarily be won.

Notes

Introduction

1. Janet Adshead, *The Study of Dance* (London: Dance Books, 1981), p. 94.
2. Michel Foucault, *Archéologie du savoir* (Paris: Gallimard, 1967).
3. Henri-Irénée Marrou, *De la connaissance historique* (Paris: Seuil, 1954).
4. Deborah Jowitt, *Time and the Dancing Image* (New York: Morrow, 1988), p. 10.
5. Jean Trudel, "La Danse traditionnelle au Québec," *Forces*, 32 (1975), p. 34.

Chapter 1

1. Paul-André Linteau et al., *Histoire du Québec contemporain: le Québec depuis 1930* (Montreal: Boréal, 1986), p. 5. Most of the socioeconomic data in this chapter comes from this volume.
2. Louis Caron, *La Vie d'artiste* (Montreal: Boréal, 1987), p. 106.
3. Jean Laflamme and Rémi Tourangeau, *L'Eglise et le théâtre au Québec* (Montreal: Fides, 1979), p. 276.
4. Gérard Morisset, "Les arts dans la province du Québec," *Commission royale d'enquête sur l'avancement des arts, des lettres et des sciences au Canada* (Ottawa: Government of Canada, 1940), p. 393.
5. Renée Legris et al., *Le Théâtre au Québec 1825–1980* (Montreal: VLB, 1988). Most of the information in this paragraph comes from this book.
6. *Ibid.*, p. 6.
7. Trudel, "La danse traditionnelle au Québec," p. 42.
8. Robert Lionel Séguin, *La Danse traditionnelle au Québec* (Quebec: Presses de l'Université du Québec, 1986), p. 39.
9. *Ibid.*
10. Laflamme, *L'Eglise et le théâtre au Québec*, p. 70.
11. *Ibid.*, p. 73.
12. *Ibid.*, p. 126.
13. *Ibid.*
14. *Ibid.*, p. 196.
15. *Ibid.*, p. 229.
16. Séguin, *La Danse traditionelle au Québec*, pp. 55-56.
17. Michael Crabb and Andrew Oxenham, *Dance Today in Canada* (Toronto: Simon and Pierre, 1977), p. 6.
18. Séguin, *La Danse traditionnelle au Québec*, p. 37.
19. Mary Jane Warner, "Theatrical Dancing in Pre-Confederation Toronto," *Canadian Dance Studies*, 1 (1994), p. 16.
20. *La Presse*, 2 January 1900, p. 5.
21. *La Presse*, 3 January 1905, p. 5.
22. "Ezzak Ruvenoff Who Brought the Dance to Canada, Dies," *The Montreal Star*, 8 June 1970, p. 52.

Chapter II

1. For the social and political background during this period, see Linteau, *Histoire du Québec contemporain*.
2. *Radio Monde*, 27 September 1941.
3. Francis Coleman, "Ballet in Canada," *The Dancing Times*, November 1945, p. 63.

Chapter III

1. Linteau, *l'Histoire du Québec contemporain*, p. 27.

2. "Choromanski compare le roman à l'entrevue," *La Presse*, n.d.
3. Louis Bédard, *Le Droit*, 22 October 1949.

Chapter IV

1. Michel Landry, "Situation de la danse au Québec: Prologue," *Réflex*, 2, no. 4 (1982), p. 11.
2. Anna Kisselgoff, "Has the Dance Boom Run its Course?" *The New York Times*, 3 May 1985, and "Faith, Death, and a Swivel Chair," *The New York Times*, 15 April 1988.

Chapter V

1. Laurent Mailhot and Benoît Melançon, "Littérature, Nation, Etat," *L'Etat et la culture* (Quebec City: IQRC, 1986), p. 61.
2. Esther Trépanier, "L'émergence d'un discours de la modernité dans la critique d'art," *L'Avènement de la modernité culturelle au Québec* (Quebec City: IQRC, 1984), p. 102. In the original, the interviewee's words are in English; the author's comments, in French.
3. Quoted in Claude Gosselin, *Françoise Sullivan: Rétrospective* (Quebec City: Ministère des Affaires culturelles, 1981), p. 49.
4. Jean Basile, "Le Groupe de la Place Royale," *Le Devoir*, 10 March 1967.
5. Quoted in Jacques Thériault, "Etre de son temps et authentique," *Le Devoir*, 23 March 1968.
6. Portions of this section appear in the author's article, "Groupe Nouvelle Aire: Why it Must Survive: A Personal View," *Dance in Canada*, Winter 1983, pp. 7-12.

Chapter VI

1. Jocelyne Lepage, "Pour combler le vide des années 30," *La Presse*, 24 October 1987.

Chapter VII

1. Quoted in the souvenir program for "Les Jeunes Montréalais," presented by Les Grands Ballets Canadiens at the Place des Arts, 12 March 1987.

Chapter VIII

1. Angèle Dagenais, "Printemps et danse à Montréal," *Le Devoir*, 24 March 1980.

Chapter X

1. Yves Taschereau, "Danse Québec Danse," *Maclean*, December 1975, p. 36.
2. Guy Scarpeta, *L'Impureté*, 1(Paris: Grasset, 1985).

Selected Bibliography

General Reference Works

Baillargeon, Jean-Paul. *Les pratiques culturelles des Québécois: une autre image de nous-mêmes*. Québec: Institut Québecois de Recherche sur la Culture, 1986.

Bissonnette, Lise, ed. "Les Créateurs: forces vives de notre Société." *Forces*, 84 (Winter 1989), pp. 1-80. [Trans. by Amtra as "The Creators: The Driving Forces of Our Society."]

Borduas, Paul-Emile, et al. *Refus Global: recueil de textes*. Montreal: Henri Tranquille, 1948.

Bourassa, André G., and Gilles Lapointe. *Refus Global et ses environs*. L'Hexagone. Gouvernement du Québec: Ministère des Affaires culturelles du Québec, 1988.

Brown, Craig, ed. *The Illustrated History of Canada*. Toronto: Lester Orpen Dennys, 1987.

Canadian Encyclopedia. 3 vols. Edmonton: Hurtig, 1985.

Caron, Louis. *La Vie d'artiste*. Montreal: Boréal, 1987.

Foucault, Michel. *Archéologie du savoir*. Paris: Gallimard, 1969.

Laflamme, Jean, and Rémi Tourangeau. *L'Eglise et le théâtre au Québec*. Montreal: Fides, 1979.

Lamonde, Yvan, and Esther Trépanier. *L'Avènement de la modernité culturelle au Québec*. Québec: Institut Québecois de Recherche sur la Culture, 1986.

LeGoff, Jacques, ed. *La Nouvelle Histoire*. Les Encyclopédies du savoir moderne. Paris: Rezt, 1978.

Legris, Renée, Jean-Marc Lavoie, André Bourassa, and Gilbert David. *Le Théâtre au Québec, 1825-1980*. Montreal: VLB, 1988.

Levasseur, Roger. *Loisir et culture au Québec*. Montreal: Boréal, 1982.

Linteau, P.A., R. Durocher, J.C. Robert, and F. Picard. *Histoire du Québec contemporain: le Québec depuis 1930*. Montreal: Boréal, 1986.

Mailhot, Laurent, and Benoît Melançon. *L'Etat et la culture*. Québec: Institut Québécois de Recherche sur la Culture, 1986.

Marietti, Angèle K. *Michel Foucault: archéologie et généalogie*. Rev. ed. Paris: Livre de Poche, 1985.

Marrou, Henri-Irénée. *De la connaissance historique*. Collection Points. Paris: Seuil, 1954.

Mathews, Robin. *Canadian Identity: Major Forces Shaping the Life of a People*. Ottawa: Steel Rail Publishing, 1988.

McCourt, Edward. "Canadian Letters." In *Recueil de quelques études spéciales, Commission Royale d'enquête sur l'avancement des arts, des lettres et des sciences au Canada 1949-1950*, pp. 67-82. Ottawa: Gouvernement du Canada, 1950.

Morisset, Gérard. "Les arts dans la province de Québec." In *Recueil de quelques études spéciales, Commission Royale d'enquête sur l'avancement des arts, des lettres et des sciences au Canada 1949-1950*, pp. 393-405. Ottawa: Gouvernement du Canada, 1950.

Parent, Alphone Marie. *Commission royale d'enquête sur l'enseignement dans la province de Québec: Commission Parent*. 5 vols. Québec: Imprimerie Pierre Des Marais, 1963.

Rioux, Marcel. *Rapport de la Commission d'enquête sur l'enseignement des arts au Québec*. 4 vols. Québec: Editeur officiel du Québec, 1968.

Royal Commission Studies: A Selection of Essays Prepared for the Royal Commission on National Development in the Arts, Letters and Sciences 1949-1951. Ottawa: Government of Canada, 1951.

Sandwell, B.K. "Present Day Influences on Canadian Society." In *Recueil de quelques études spéciales, Commission Royale d'enquête surl'avancement des arts, des lettres et des sciences au Canada 1949-1950*, pp. 1-11. Ottawa: Gouvement du Canada, 1950.

Scarpetta, Guy. *L'Impureté*. Paris: Grasset, 1985.

Books on Dance

Adshead, Janet. *The Study of Dance*. London: Dance Books, 1981.

Adshead, Janet, ed. *Dance Analysis: Theory and Practice*. London: Dance Books, 1988.

Adshead, Janet, and June Layson. *Dance History: A Methodology for Study*. London: Dance Books, 1983.

Bell, Ken, and Celia Franca. *The National Ballet of Canada*. Toronto: University of Toronto Press, 1978.

Chujoy, Anatole, and P.W. Manchester, eds. *The Dance Encyclopedia*. Rev. ed. New York: Simon and Schuster, 1962.

Collier, Clifford, and Pierre Guilmette. *Ressources sur la danse dans les bibliothèques canadiennes*. Ottawa: Bibliothèque Nationale du Canada, Division de l'inventaire des ressources, 1982.

Conte, Michel. *Nu comme dans un nuage*. Montreal: Edition de la Montagne, 1980.

Crabb, Michael, ed. *Visions: Ballet and its Future*. Essays from the International Dance Conference to commemorate the twenty-fifth anniversary of The National Ballet of Canada. Toronto: Simon and Pierre, 1978.

Crabb, Michael, and Andrew Oxenham. *Dance Today in Canada*. Toronto: Simon and Pierre, 1977.

"Dancing": A Journal Devoted to Terpsichore: Art, Physical Culture and Fashionable Entertainment. London: R.M. Crompton, 1891, May 1893. Reprint. Toronto: Press of Terpsichore, 1984.

Dubuc, Jacques. *Le langage corporel dans la liturgie*. Montreal: Fides, 1986.

Febvre, Michèle. *La danse au défi*. Montreal: Parachute, 1987.

Foster, Susan Leigh. *Reading Dancing: Bodies and Subjects in Contemporary American Dance*. Berkeley: University of California Press, 1986.

Germain, Victorin (Abbé). *Dansera-t-on chez moi? Un cas de conscience*. Québec: Presses de l'action sociale Itée, 1930.

Guilmette, Pierre. *Bibliographie de la danse théâtrale au Canada*. Ottawa: Bibliothèque Nationale du Canada, 1970.

Jackson, Graham. *Dance as Dance: Selected Reviews and Essays*. Ottawa: Catalyst, 1978.

Jowitt, Deborah. *Time and the Dancing Image*. New York: Morrow, 1988.

Koegler, Horst, ed. *The Concise Oxford Dictionary of Ballet*. Rev. ed. London: Oxford University Press, 1982.

Lacasse, Adelard. *La danse apprise chez soi*. Montreal: Imprimerie Moderne, 1918.

Leborgne, Odette. *Un pas vers les autres*. Montreal: Editions du Jour, 1976.

Lorrain, Roland. *A moi ma chair, à moi mon âme: du cloître au ballet*. Montreal: VLB, 1985.

Lorrain, Roland. *Les Grands Ballets Canadiens ou cette femme qui nous fit danser*. Montreal: Editions du Jour, 1973.

Mitchell, Lillian Leonore. "Boris Volkoff: Dancer, Teacher, Choreographer." Ph.D. diss., University of Michigan, 1985.

Picard, René. *La Danse au Canada*. Document No. 63. Ottawa: Government of Canada, Ministry of Foreign Affairs, 1984.

Robinson, Jacqueline. *L'aventure de la danse moderne en France (1920-1970)*. Collection Sources. Paris: Bougé, 1990.

Séguin, Robert Lionel. *La Danse traditionnelle au Québec*. Québec: Presses de l'Université du Québec, 1986.

Serre, Jean-Claude, ed. *La Recherche en danse: actes du colloque international de la Sorbonne*. Paris: Chiron, 1986.

Souvenir program of *Festival International de Nouvelle Danse*. Montreal: Parachute, 1985.

Souvenir program of *Festival International de Nouvelle Danse*. Montreal: Parachute, 1987.

Souvenir program of *Festival International de Nouvelle Danse*. Montreal: Parachute, 1989.

Sullivan, Françoise. *Rétrospective*. Québec: Ministère des Affaires Culturelles du Québec, 1981.

"Survey of Canada." *Dance Magazine*. Special issue on Canadian dance. Apr. 1971.

Taplin, Diana Theodores, ed. *New Directions in Dance*. Ontario: Pergamon Press, 1979.

Valois, Marcel. *Figures de danse*. Montreal: Les Editions Variétés, 1943.

Wyman, Max. *Dance Canada: An Illustrated History*. Vancouver: Douglas McIntyre, 1989.

———. *The Royal Winnipeg Ballet: The First Forty Years*. Toronto: Doubleday, 1978.

Articles

Albert, Mathieu. "Les débuts de Montréal Danse: un diaporama sec." *Le Devoir*, 28 Feb. 1987.

———. "Quelques tendances." In souvenir program of *Festival International de Nouvelle Danse*, pp. 26-28. Montreal: Parachute, 1987.

Anderson, Jack. "Style, Flair, Conviction." *Dance Magazine*, Mar. 1977, pp. 20-21.

Asselin, Suzanne. "Edouard Lock et le La La La Human Steps: il dérange, bouscule et séduit." *La Presse*, 11 July 1987.

———. "Howard Richard et Danseurs: la valeur n'attend pas le nombre des années, au théâtre D.B. Clarke." *Le Devoir*, 4 Mar. 1985, p. 5.

———. "Léveillé à fleur de peau." *Le Devoir*, 13 Feb. 1982, p. 26.

———. "Paul-André Fortier: danser ce que vit le monde." *Le Devoir*, 6 Feb. 1982.

———. "Qui Danse?" *Dance in Canada*, Winter 1977, p. 7.

"L'atelier de chorégraphie à la Boutique d'opéra." *La Presse*, 29 Nov. 1963, p. 9.

"Au bénéfice des Ballets Métropolitains." *La Presse*, 22 Sept. 1966, p. 25.

"Avec Balanchine, un autre spécialiste viendra étudier la situation du ballet dans notre pays: le critique anglais Buckle." *La Presse*, 5 Feb. 1962, p. 19.

"Ballerine montréalaise à Londres." *La Presse*, 2 Feb. 1961, p. 6.

"Le ballet amateur: art idéal pour acquérir une belle démarche." *La Presse*, 15 Sept. 1961, p. 16.

"Le ballet de B. Macdonald bien reçu à Leningrad." *La Presse*, 2 July 1963, p. 27.

"Un ballet d'envergure composé des Grands Ballets Canadiens." *La Presse*, 15 Apr. 1959, p. 30.

"Ballet Festival Scores in Canada." *Dance News*, June 1948, p. 3.

Barnes, Clive. "Margie Gillis: Canada's Gift to Dance Recital." *New York Post*, 17 Feb. 1986.

Basile, Jean. "Le Groupe de la Place Royale." *Le Devoir*, 10 Mar. 1967.

"Beauty in Motion." *The Montrealer*, Apr. 1950.

Bédard, Louis. "Les Ballets Ruth Sorel: idiome moderne et poésie." *Le Droit*, 22 Oct. 1949.

"Biographical Note: Brian Macdonald." *Dance Magazine*, Oct. 1967, p. 82.

Boivin, René O. "'Figures de danse,' une oeuvre aimable par son style simple et le pittoresque de son récit." *Radio-Monde*, 1 May 1943, p. 7.

Boucher, Denise. "Le centre d'art estival '63.'" *La Presse*, 29 June 1963, p. 22.

Bourassa, André G. "Danse au Québec et Modernité." In souvenir program of *Festival International de Nouvelle Danse*, pp. 16-28. Montreal: Parachute, 1987.

Bozzini, Annie. "Dossier spécial sur le FIND." *Pour la Danse*, Nov. 1987, pp. 22-23.

"Brian Macdonald back from Leningrad." *Dance Magazine*, July 1963, p. 3.

Brisebois, Marcel. "La liberté de création et la quête du sens." *Le Devoir*, 14 Oct. 1989, p. 9.

Brisson, Carole. "Daniel Léveillé: chorégraphe pour le théâtre." *Réflex*, 3, no. 1 (1983), pp. 24-25.

"Canada." *Ballet Today*, Dec. 1955, p. 8.

"Canada Festival Opens March 2." *Dance News*, Feb. 1949, p. 9.

"Canada to Run Dance Festival." *Dance News*, Apr. 1948, p. 3.

"Canadian Dance Teachers Association." *Dance News*, Feb. 1950, p. 14.

"Canadian Dance Festival." *Dance Magazine*, May 1954, p. 3.

"Canadian Festival December 17 at 4." *Dance News*, Dec. 1949, pp. 1-6.

"Canadian Festival Due in October." *Dance News*, Jan. 1950, p. 7.

"Canadian Festival Selects Companies." *Dance News*, Aug. 1950, p. 2.

"Canadian Festival Set for November 20." *Dance News*, Nov. 1950, p. 3.

"Canadian Festival to Begin November 20." *Dance News*, Oct. 1950, p. 3.

"Canadian Headlines." *Dance Magazine*, July 1955, p. 79.

Chodan, Lucinda. "From Ballet to Avant-garde: Montreal is Dance City." *The Gazette*, 18 Jan. 1986, p. D7.

"Choreographer of Our Day: Heino Heiden." *Ballet Today*, Mar. 1964, pp. 13-17.

Chujoy, Anatole. "Canada Hosts Sixth Northeastern Festival." *Dance News*, June 1965.

———. "Dance in Review: Canadian Ballet." *Dance News*, Jan. 1943.

———. "Festival is Impressive Show of Canadian Dance Talent." *Dance News*, Jan. 1951, p. 2.

"Cinq ballets par représentation au prochain festival." *La Presse*, 7 Nov. 1950, p. 18.

Citron, Paula. "Montreal's Les Grands Ballets Canadiens: The French Canadian Experience." *Dance Magazine*, Apr. 1982, pp. 62-69.

———. "New Choreography at Place des Arts." *Canadian Dance News*, 2, no. 7 (May 1982), p. 11.

———. "The Well Choreographed Montreal Dance Explosion." *Performing Arts in Canada*, Summer 1982, pp. 38-42.

Coleman, Francis. "Ballet in Canada." *The Dancing Times*, Nov. 1945, p. 63.

———. "Morenoff Ballet Music-Hall." *Dance Magazine*, June 1945, p. 35.

———. "News from Canada." *Dance Magazine*, Nov. 1957, p. 97.

"Convention in Vancouver." *Dance Magazine*, Sept. 1958, p. 5.

Crabb, Michael. "Coming of Age: 25 Years of Canadian Dance." *Performing Arts in Canada*, Nov. 1986, pp. 20-22.

———. "Dancers Should Look for the Stars Not Contemplate Their Artistic Navels." *Performing Arts Magazine*, Autumn 1974, pp. 35-37.

———. "Whither Canadian Dance History?" In *New Directions in Dance*, ed. Diana T. Taplin, pp. 97-105. Ontario: Pergamon Press, 1979.

Crabb, Michael, et al. "The Brinson Report: The Community Responds. Profile: The Schools, The Future? Other Views." *Dance in Canada*, Winter 1976, pp. 1-28.

"Création d'un ballet inspiré de notre folklore." *La Presse*, 10 Oct. 1959.

Dagenais, Angèle. "Entre Six: 5 ans, 500 représentations." *Le Devoir*, 8 Apr. 1979.

———. "Entre-Six: une micro-troupe aux pas de géant." *Le Devoir*, 9 Oct. 1975.

———. "Printemps et danse à Montréal." *Le Devoir*, 24 Mar. 1980.

"Dancer's Employment Forces Cancellation of Festival." *Dance News*, Apr. 1955, p. 5.

"Danse contemporaine: Birouté Nagys." *La Presse*, 5 Dec. 1959, p. 32.

"La danse moderne à l'Egrégore." *La Presse*, 7 Mar. 1967, p. 25.

"Début canadien de Margaret Mercier." *La Presse*, 16 Apr. 1959, p. 34.

De Repentigny, Françoise. "Plastique de la danse en termes de formes et de lignes." *La Presse*, 12 June 1961, p. 6.

De Repentigny, Rodolphe. "Eric Hyrst danse malgré une blessure." *La Presse*, 18 Apr. 1959.

Desjardins, Maurice. "Choromanski compare le roman à l'entrevue." *La Presse*, n.d.

Dufresne, Jean. "Les petites fées de l'aiguille vont au bal." *La Presse*, 21 Nov. 1959, p. 45.

"Editor Covers Canadian Fete." *Dance News*, Dec. 1950, p. 1.

"Elizabeth Leese." In *The Dance Encyclopedia*, ed. Anatole Chujoy and P.W. Manchester, pp. 565-566. Rev. ed. New York: Simon and Schuster, 1962.

"Elizabeth Leese." *Dance News*, Oct. 1962, pp. 13, 15.

"Elizabeth Leese dies in Montreal." *Dance News*, Sept. 1962, p. 13.

"Ezzak Ruvenoff Who Brought the Dance to Canada, Dies." *The Montreal Star*, 8 June 1970, p. 52.

"Fernand Nault, Choreographer for Montreal Theatre Ballet." *Dance Magazine*, Mar. 1958, p. 4.

"Fernand Nault en URSS avec le Ballet Théâtre." *La Presse*, 1 June 1966, p. 49.

"Fifteen Canadian Ballet Companies to Appear at Festival in Montreal." *Dance Magazine*, Aug. 1950, p. 34.

Gélinas, Aline. "Les ambitions de Howard Richard: créer des oeuvres accessibles." *La Presse*, 6 Apr. 1985, p. D8.

————. "Les ambitions de Montréal Danse: les autres n'ont rien à craindre." *La Presse*, 31 Jan. 1987.

————. "La danse d'ici." *Forces*, 84 (Winter 1989), pp. 45- 47. [Trans. by Amtra as "Dance in Quebec."]

————. "La danse vue d'ailleurs." *Vice Versa*, 25 (Dec. 1988).

————. "Jean-Pierre Perreault Chorégraphe." *Réflex*, 5, no. 22 (1985), pp. 14-19.

————. "Paysage actuel de la danse à Montréal: alternatives théâtrales: Canada et Québec 86." *Repères*, 26 (Sept. 1986), pp. 63-77.

————. "Les premiers pas de Montréal Danse: quand un art devient populaire, attention." *La Presse*, 7 Feb. 1987.

Germain, Georges Hébert. "E.T. et ses stars." *L'Actualité*, Sept. 1985, pp. 42-49.

Glueck, Grace. "Clashing Views Reshape Art History." *The New York Times*, 20 Dec. 1987.

Gillis, Margie. "Parting the Bamboo Curtain: Margie Gillis in China." *Dance in Canada*, Winter 1979, pp. 22-23.

Gingras, Claude. "Un ballet sur un texte de Pierre Bourgault." *La Presse*, 2 Sept. 1967, p. 27.

————. "Décevante, cette 'Rose Latulippe.'" *La Presse*, 30 Aug. 1967, p. 80.

————. "Excellent début de l'atelier de chorégraphie." *La Presse*, 9 Dec. 1963, p. 24.

————. "Expériences musicales et chorégraphiques." *La Presse*, 11 Sept. 1967, p. 60.

————. "Le Groupe de danse moderne à l'Egrégore." *La Presse*, 10 Feb. 1964, p. 9.

————. "Le groupe de Jeanne Renaud; déjà, du style." *La Presse*, 9 Mar. 1967, p. 30.

————. "Un groupe en perte de vitesse." *La Presse*, 11 Feb. 1965, p. 11.

Girard, Jacques. "De la danse magique aux Sylphides." *Le Quartier Latin*, 11 Oct. 1960, pp. 4-5.

Glover, Guy. "Reflections on Canadian ballet." *Canadian Art*, 8 (Spring 1951), pp. 115-119.

Godfrey, Stephen. "A Step Ahead of the Others: The Visual, Experimental Excite Montreal Choreographers, Fans." *The Globe and Mail*, 10 Mar. 1990.

Goodman, Saul. "Margaret Mercier." *Dance Magazine*, Dec. 1962, pp. 48-49.

"Le Groupe de danse moderne." *La Presse*, 8 Feb. 1965, p. 15.

"Le Groupe Gets Canadian Grant." *Dance News*, Nov. 1967, p. 6.

Guilmette, Pierre. "Critique." *Nouvelles chorégraphiques du Canada Français*, 1 (15 Feb. 1964), p. 3.

————. "Lettre ouverte à 'De la danse magique aux Sylphides,' par Jacques Girard." *Le Quartier Latin*, 15 Nov. 1960.

————. "Problèmes de la critique de danse." *Nouvelles chorégraphiques du Canada Français*, 2 (1 Apr. 1964), pp. 6-9.

Gallant, Mavis. "Progressive School." *The Standard*, 22 June 1946, pp. 15-17.

Heller, Zelda. "Who's Killing Modern Dance?" *The Montreal Star*, 3 May 1969.

"Here and There in Canada." *Dance Magazine*, Jan. 1956, p. 87.

Hering, Doris. "Reviewer's Stand." *Dance Magazine*, Feb. 1950, p. 44.

————. "Sixth Canadian Ballet Festival." *Dance Magazine*, July 1954, pp. 14, 19, 44, 45.

————. "'Walk Soft': Some Trends, Positive and Otherwise, Among the Regional Ballet Companies." *Dance Magazine*, Jan. 1960, pp. 56-57.

Hicklin, Ralph. "Les Grands Ballets Canadiens: A Certain Inadequacy." *Saturday Night*, 12 May 1962, pp. 30-31.

Howe-Beck, Linde. "Eddy Toussaint: Cultural Champion of Dance in Quebec." *Dance in Canada*, Spring 1982, pp. 14-16.

————. "Eddy Toussaint's Ballet de Montréal: A Company of Consequence." *Dance Magazine*, Feb. 1985, pp. 56-64.

————. "Eddy Toussaint's Ballet de Montréal at 15." *Dance in Canada*, Winter 1989, pp. 18-23.

————. "Gillis Superb, Leaves Viewers Limp." *The Gazette*, 18 Feb. 1980.

————. "Les Grands Ballets at 30: Celebration and Crisis Management Vie for Centre Stage." *Dance in Canada*, Summer 1988, pp. 7-13.

————. "Have Dance, Will Travel: Choreographer Brian Macdonald a Cultural Whirlwind." *The Gazette*, 1 Feb. 1986.

————. "Qui Danse?" *The Gazette*, 10 June 1979.

————. "Qui Danse?" *The Gazette*, 12 May 1980.

————. "Richard Dances Show His Versatility." *The Gazette*, 16 Feb. 1989.

————. "The State of Dance in Montreal: Restless." *The Gazette*, 6 Sept. 1986, pp. K2-K3.

————. "The State of Dance in Montreal: Terpsichore is Restless." *Dance in Canada*, Winter 1986-1987, pp. 19-21.

"In the News: Brian Macdonald." *Dance Magazine*, Dec. 1963, p. 46.

Jasmin, Claude. "Stravinsky et la danse." *La Presse*, 31 Aug. 1963, p. 19.

Johnson, Sydney. "The Choreography of Sensibility, Divorced from Emotion." *The Montreal Star*, 14 Sept. 1968, p. 20.

————. "Montreal and Modern Dance: It Went Thataway 30 Years Ago." *The Montreal Star*, 23 Apr. 1966.

————. "Recital by Dance Club at McGill." *The Montreal Star*, Feb. 1959.

Johnstone, Kenneth. "The Dance in Canada." *Dance News Annual*, 1953, pp. 158-166.

Jowitt, Deborah. "Dance." *The Village Voice*, 26 Nov. 1985.

Katz Rosenbaum, Beverly. "Canadian Dance: What Makes the Dance Community in Canada Unique?" *Dance in Canada*, Summer 1987, pp. 31-36.

Keable, Jacques. "Quand la danse est produite à un rythme industriel." *La Presse*, 29 Feb. 1964, p. 11.

Kisselgoff, Anna. "Les Ballets Jazz Makes New York Debut." *The New York Times*, 22 Feb. 1978.

————. "Dance in Montreal, Experimental Troupes." *The New York Times*, 30 Sept. 1985.

————. "The Dance: Montreal's Margie Gillis." *The New York Times*, 12 Feb. 1986.

————. "Faith, Death, and a Swivel Chair." *The New York Times*, 15 Apr. 1988.

————. "Has the Dance Boom Run its Course?" *The New York Times*, 3 May 1985.

————. "In Montreal, A New Electricity Is in the Air." *The New York Times*. 13 Mar. 1988.

Knelman, Martin. "The King of Crossover." *Saturday Night*, July 1985, pp. 38-39.

Koegler, Horst, ed. "Ruth Abramowitsch (Sorel)." In *The Concise Oxford Dictionary of Ballet*, p. 1. London: Oxford University Press, 1977.

Landry, Michel. "Situation de la danse au Québec: Prologue." *Réflex*, 2, no. 4 (1982), pp. 10-11.

Leddiak, David. "Conversation with Fernand Nault." *Dance Magazine*, Apr. 1960, pp. 16-17.

Lefebvre, Paul, and Denis Marleau. "Des spectacles qui nous viennent du corps: la danse-théâtre au Québec." *Jeu* (special dance issue), Dec. 1984, pp. 40-73.

Léger, Micheline. "East of Egypt: l'univers des rêves de Montanaro." *Réflex*, 5, no. 24 (1985), pp. 4-7.

Lepage, Jocelyne. "Pour combler le vide des années 30." *La Presse*, 24 Oct. 1987.

Lorrain, Roland. "Le ballet n'est pas le refuge des 'hommelets.'" *Le Petit Journal*, 17 May 1953.

————. "Grossière incompétence dans les écoles de ballet." *Le Petit Journal*, 19 Apr. 1953.

————. "Ignorance du ballet chez l'élite montréalaise." *Le Petit Journal*, 3 May 1953, p. 73.

————. "La niaiserie de la danse de ballet à Montréal." *Le Petit Journal*, 12 Apr. 1953.

————. "Propos sur une déesse négligée." *Le Devoir*, 11 Mar. 1961.

————. "Le refoulement est le premier ennemi de l'art véritable." *Le Petit Journal*, 24 May 1953, p. 78.

Louppe, Laurence. "A Nouvelle France, Nouvelle Danse." *Libération*, 4 Oct. 1988.

"Macdonald à Winnipeg." *La Presse*, 17 Mar. 1964, p. 21.

"Margaret Mercier et Eric Hyrst aux Grands Ballets." *La Presse*, 11 Feb. 1961, p. 19.

"Mariage de Margaret Mercier." *La Presse*, 4 May 1965, p. 33.

Marinoff, Sergei. "I Can Teach You to Dance Like This." *Dance Lover Magazine*, Dec. 1923.

Maynard, Olga. "Ballet in Canada Today: Ludmilla Chiriaeff and Les Grands Ballets Canadiens." *Dance Magazine*, Apr. 1971, pp. 56-64.

————. "Les Ballets Jazz Dance Le Style Québécois." *Dance Magazine*, Jan. 1974, pp. 72-74.

McLain Stoop, Norma. "The Canadian Cosmopolitan: Montreal's Brian Macdonald." *Dance Magazine*, Mar. 1984, pp. 63-65.

"Michael Montanaro: un homme de la Renaissance dans l'univers chorégraphique des années 80." *Tendances*, Centre National des Arts, Jan. 1987.

Michel, Marcelle. "Danse: au Festival International de Nouvelle Danse. La Nouvelle Danse qu'est ce que c'est?" *Le Monde*, 16 Oct. 1985, p. 15.

"Montreal Has Dance Series." *Dance News*, May 1949, p. 3.

"National Ballet Company and Heino Heiden." *The Dancing Times*, 544 (1956), p. 235.

"Note biographique." *La Presse*, 15 Aug. 1963, p. 14.

"Le nouveau ballet d'Elizabeth Leese." *La Presse*, 15 June 1955, p. 38.

Officer, Jillian. "The Growth of Dance in Canada." In *Contemporary Canadian Theater: New World Visions*, ed. Anton Wagner, pp. 262-273. Toronto: Simon and Pierre, 1985.

————. *The Original Ballets Appearing in the Repertoire of Les Ballets Chiriaeff 1955-1958 and Les Grands Ballets Canadiens 1958-1980*. Report of a research project funded by The Canada Council. Waterloo: University of Waterloo, 1982.

Panet-Raymond, Silvy. "New Currents in Montreal: Innocence and Irreverence in La Belle Metropole." *Dance in Canada*, Summer 1981, pp. 3-6.

————. "1948-1984: quelque part dans l'histoire de percevoir." *Interventions*, Spring 1984.

Picard, René. "Danse Portrait: Jean-Pierre Perreault." *Réflex*, 3, no. 1 (1983), pp. 21-22.

————. "Esquisse de la danse moderne au Québec." *L"Interdit*, Feb. 1974, pp. 4-5.

————. "T'appelles ça vivre toé, Joe ?" *Réflex*, 5, no. 21 (1985), p. 14.

"Le premier ballet en Nouvelle France." *La Presse*, 27 Feb. 1967, p. 17.

"Quebec Teachers Present Festival." *Dance News*, Apr. 1956, p. 10.

"Quebec Teachers Present Forum." *Dance News*, Jan. 1956, p. 9.

"Quel est l'avenir du ballet au Canada?" *La Presse*, 28 Sept. 1961, p. 18.

"RA." *The Standard*, 29 Apr. 1944.

Renaud, Jeanne. "Point of View: Artistic Vision for Canada's Major Ballet Companies." *Dance in Canada*, Winter 1987, pp. 23-24.

"Richard Buckle critique au Sunday Times London." *La Presse*, 2 Feb. 1962, p. 20.

Rioux, Christian. "Flyée: puisant à la fois dans le classique et le contemporain, Louise Lecavalier est le prototype de la danseuse des années 80." *L'Actualité*, Apr. 1989, pp. 154-158.

Roberge, François. "La vraie vie de la danse à Montréal." *Le Devoir*, 26 May 1978, p. 4.

"Rose LaTulippe, A Canadian Legend and Ballet, With Marking Notes From the Diary of its Choreographer, Macdonald." *Dance Magazine*, Dec. 1966, pp. 58-62.

Schmidt, Jochen. "Montréal: As Young and as New as Possible." *Ballett International*, Dec. 1987, p. 32.

Siskind, Jacob. "The Nudies Have Come!" *The Gazette*, 3 July 1970, p. 18.

"Spectacle des Ballets Métropolitains." *La Presse*, 12 May 1966.

"Spectacle 1959 de l'Ecole Morenoff." *La Presse*, 16 May 1959, p. 52.

St.-Germain, Pierre. "Des Montréalais créent le premier ballet Canadien." *Le Petit Journal*, 23 Jan. 1949.

Stratyner, Barbara Naomi Cohen, ed. "Ruth Abramowitz (Sorel)." In *Biographical Dictionary of the Dance*. New York: Dance Horizons, 1982.

Stahle, Anna Greta. "Brian Macdonald Leaves Swedish Ballet at Year End." *Dance News*, Jan. 1967, p. 5.

Sorell, Walter. "Modern Dance Festival in Toronto." *Dance Magazine*, May 1963, pp. 16, 63.

"Subvention de la Commission du Centenaire pour la création du ballet 'Rose LaTulippe.'" *La Presse*, 27 June 1966, p. 20.

Taschereau, Yves. "Nous on veut danser: Danse, Québec, Danse." *Maclean*, Dec. 1975, pp. 30-36.

Taplin, Diana Theodores. "Choreographers in Process: 1975: Lawrence Gradus." *Dance in Canada*, Winter 1976, pp. 21-23.

Tasso, Lily. "Une nouvelle compagnie montréalaise: les Ballets Métropolitains." *La Presse*, 31 May 1965, p. 15.

Tembeck, Iro. "A la recherche du faune perdu de Nijinski." In *Corps témoin: bilan de la danse, saison 1989-1990*, pp. 33-34. Montréal: Les Herbes Rouges, 1992.

————. "Les Ballets Jazz de Montréal Brightens the World: French Canadian Troupe Going Strong at Fifteen." *The World and I*, Aug. 1987, pp. 208-212.

————. "Courants chorégraphiques actuels dans la danse moderne québecoise." *Réflex*, 2, no. 1 (1982), pp. 15-18.

————. "La danse: parente pauvre des arts et paria de notre culture." In *Les pratiques culturelles des Québécois, une autre image de nous-mêmes*, pp. 183-214. Québec: Institut Québécois de Recherche sur la Culture, 1986.

————. "Four Decades of Modern Dance in Quebec: Maintaining a Steady Independence from Tradition." In *Proceedings of the CORD Conference in Toronto* (1988), pp. 191-207.

————. "Groupe Nouvelle Aire: rétrospective d'une ère passée." *Réflex* 3, no. 1 (1983), pp. 7-11.

————. "La La La Human Steps." *Banff Letters*, Spring 1986, pp. 58-60.

————. "Montréal dansait-elle à l'aube du Refus Global." In *Brochure commémorative de la reconstruction du Récital de Danse de 1948 de Françoise Sullivan et Jeanne Renaud*, pp. 7-9. Montreal: Musée d'Art Contemporain, 1988.

————. "Montreal International Festival of New Dance: From Neo-Expressionism to Neo-Romanticism." *Dance in Canada*, Winter 1985-1986, pp. 14-17.

————. "New Dance in Quebec." *Dance in Canada*, Summer 1984, pp. 49-52.

————. "Petite histoire de la danse moderne au Québec." *Réflex*, 4, no. 2 (1984), pp. 23-29.

————. "Playing Musical Chairs: Identity Crises in the Montreal Dance Community." *Dance in Canada*, Summer 1987, pp. 23- 28.

————. "Politics and Dance: A Case Study of the Maginot Line Separating Francophone and Anglophone Dance Artists in Montréal." In *Proceedings of the Hong Kong International Dance Conference* (1990), vol. 2, pp. 260-273.

————. "Terpsichore's Growth in Quebec and Other Provinces of Canada: A Comparison." *CAHPER* (special dance issue), June 1989, pp. 7-12.

Thériault, Jacques. "Etre de son temps et authentique." *Le Devoir*, 23 Mar. 1968, p. 13.

Thibault, Michèle. "Margie Gillis, seule en scène de Montréal à Pékin, de New York à Paris." *La Presse*, 14 Nov. 1980.

"The Third Canadian Ballet Festival: Ruthanna Boris at Seville Theatre." *Dance Magazine*, Nov. 1950, p. 48.

Thistle, Lauretta. "Sorel Ballet Company: In Pleasing Presentation." *The Ottawa Citizen*, 22 Oct. 1949.

Trépanier, Esther. "L'Emergence d'un discours sur la modernité dans la critique d'art." In *L'Avènement de la modernité culturelle au Québec*, ed. Yvan Lamonde and Esther Trépanier. Québec: Institut Québécois de Recherche sur la Culture, 1986.

Tourangeau, Jean. "Le post-modernisme au Québec: aspects sur le Québec." *Journal of Canadian Studies*, 23, no. 4 (1989), pp. 70-80.

Trudel, Jean. "La Danse traditionnelle au Québec." *Forces*, 32 (1975), pp. 34-43.

Valois, Marcel. "André Ménard parle de la danse à Paris." *La Presse*, 14 Oct. 1950, p. 59.

————. "Danseurs canadiens qui rivalisent avec ceux de l'étranger." *La Presse*, 24 Nov. 1950.

————. "Des danseurs de chez nous à l'étranger." *La Presse*, 23 June 1950, p. 41.

————. "M. David Yeddeau a la tâche ardue pour le festival du ballet." *La Presse*, 20 Nov. 1950, p. 24.

————. "De portée nationale." *La Presse*, 18 Nov. 1950, p. 61.

————. "Deux troupes ont fait leurs débuts au His Majesty's." *La Presse*, 23 Nov. 1950, p. 38.

————. "Deuxième spectacle d'une haute qualité également partagée." *La Presse*, 22 Nov. 1950, p. 32.

————. "L'enthousiasme général à la soirée d'inauguration." *La Presse*, 21 Nov. 1950, p. 24.

————. "Un festival de ballet à Montréal, il y a dix ans." *La Presse*, 23 July 1960, p. 25.

————. "Imagination dans la chorégraphie de Maurice Morenoff." *La Presse*, 5 Apr. 1948, p. 10.

————. "Des prix et des couronnes." *La Presse*, 2 Dec. 1950, pp. 61, 65.

————. "Propos sur la danse." *La Presse*, 3 Nov. 1945, p. 52.

————. "Public enthousiaste au spectacle soigné des Ballets Québec." *La Presse*, 19 May 1950, p. 23.

————. "Une semaine canadienne." *La Presse*, 7 Oct. 1950, pp. 59, 62.

————. "Le sens éducationnel du spectacle vivant de l'école." *La Presse*, 31 May 1951, p. 29.

————. "Sixième spectacle du ballet." *La Presse*, 25 Nov. 1950, p. 37.

————. "Spectacle agréable et de bonne tenue du Montréal Ballet." *La Presse*, 19 Apr. 1950, p. 29.

Vita, Kati. "Jacqueline Lemieux: 1939-1979." *Dance in Canada*, Winter 1979, p. 24.

Wagner, Thelma. "The Modern Dance." *McGill News*, Spring 1942, pp. 21-22, 52.

Warner, Mary Jane. "Theatrical Dancing in Pre-Confederation Toronto." *Canadian Dance Studies*, 1 (1994), pp. 11-26.

Whittaker, Herbert. "Brian Macdonald: A Personal View." *Dance in Canada*, Summer 1988, pp. 18-25.

————. "The Fourth Canadian Ballet Festival: A Review." *Dance Magazine*, June 1952, pp. 16-17, 33-34.

————. "From Little Acorns: A Review of the Fifth Canadian Dance Festival." *Dance Magazine*, June 1953, pp. 18-19.

Wyman, Max. "Who Needs Canadian Dance? A Futile Search for National Identity." *Dance in Canada*, Winter 1983, pp. 11-14.

Interviews Conducted by Author

Note: An asterisk (*) following an entry indicates that the interview was audiotaped.

Ballard, Stéphanie. Montreal, 18 Oct. 1988.*

Belleval Fournier, Jean de. Montreal, 27 Sept. 1988.*

Blier-Cantin, Suzanne. Montreal, 18 Jan. 1988.*

Boudot, Michel. Montreal, 9 Dec. 1987.*

Cadet-Roy, Andréa. Montreal, 10 Dec. 1987.*

Caiserman-Roth, Ghitta. Montreal, 20 Dec. 1988.*

Chiriaeff, Ludmilla. Montreal, Winter 1988, Autumn 1987.

Coleman, Christina. Montreal, 4 Jan. 1988.*

Coleman, Francis. Letter to the author, 11 Dec. 1987.

Côté, Marie. Montreal, 20 Jan. 1988.*

Crevier Gérald. Montreal, 19 July 1988.*

Desjarlais, France. Montreal, Autumn 1987.

Fischer, Juliette. Letter to the author, 24 Jan. 1988.

Flinsch, Peter. Montreal, 6 Dec. 1988.*

Fortier, Paul-André. Montreal, 31 Jan. 1989.*

Gagnier, Lise. Montreal, 16 Dec. 1987.*

Gencsy, Eva von. Montreal, 1 Dec. 1987.*

Gillis, Margie. Montreal, 18 Oct. 1988.*

Graham, Françoise. Montreal, 25 Apr. 1989.*

Haug, Martine. Montreal, Winter 1988.

Honigman, Saul. New York, June 1993.

Hyrst, Eric. Montreal, 13 Nov. 1987.*

Intini-Perreault, Vanda. Montreal, 2 Dec. 1988.*

Jackson, Daniel. Montreal, 19 Dec. 1988.*

Kon, Irene. Montreal, Winter 1989.

Lacasse-Morenoff, Maurice. Montreal, Winter 1987; Spring/Summer 1988.

Lacasse, Pierre. Montreal, Autumn 1987; Spring/Summer 1988.

Lapointe, Paul. Montreal, Autumn 1988.

Lapointe, Pierre. Sherbrooke, 11 May 1989.*

Laurin, Ginette. Montreal, 8 Dec. 1988.*

Lawrence, Emily (also known as Dorothy Manners). Montreal, Spring 1987.

Legris, Aline. Montreal, Spring 1987.

Lavalle, Josefina. Morelia (Mexico), 8 Dec. 1990.

Léveillé, Daniel. Montreal, 27 Apr. 1988.*

Macdonald, Brian. Montreal, 3 Feb. 1988.*

MacDougall, Alexander. Montreal, 14 Jan. 1988.*

Marvin, Jill. Montreal, Winter 1988.

Ménard, Thérèse. Montreal, 11 Jan. 1988.*

Millaire, Andrée. Montreal, 20 Nov. 1987.*

Montanaro, Michael. Montreal, Autumn 1988.

Moore-Ashton, Eleanor. Toronto, Jan. 1992.

Nagys, Birouté. Montreal, 28 Oct. 1988.*

Nault, Fernand. Montreal, 3 Feb. 1988.*

Paige, Brydon. Montreal, 11 Nov. 1988.*

Pauzé, Yvette. Montreal, 21 Mar. 1990.*

Pearce-Laurence, Sheila. Montreal, 8 Nov. 1988.*

Pereima, Alex. Toronto, Jan. 1992.

Perreault, Jean-Pierre. Montreal, 14 Mar. 1989.*

Peters, Anne-Marie. Montreal, 30 Nov. 1987.*

Rabin, Linda. Montreal, 12 Oct. 1989.*

Renaud, Jeanne. Montreal, 21 Jan. 1988.*

Reyna, Rosa. Morelia (Mexico), 8 Dec. 1990.

Rochon, Roger. Montreal, Autumn 1988.

Riopelle, Françoise. Montreal, 13 Sept. 1988.*

Saharuni, Randy. Montréal, 12 Jan. 1988.*

Salbaing, Genevieve. Montreal, Spring 1987.

Scott, Tom. Montreal, 26 Sept. 1988.*

Salomons Margolick, Phyllis. Montreal, Spring/Summer 1988; Autumn 1989.

Salomons Schwartz, Elsie. Montreal, 20 Aug. 1987.*

Silverstone, Ann Naran. Montreal, 15 Dec. 1988.*

Stapells, Suzanne. Telephone interview. Toronto, Feb. 1989.

Stearns, Linda. Montreal, 26 Nov. 1988.*

Sullivan, Françoise. Montreal, 15 Sept. 1988.*

Tardy, Marcus and Julia. Paris, 17 Feb. 1993.

Thom, Rose Ann. New York, June 1991.

Warren, Vincent. Montreal, 3 Nov. 1988.*

Collections

Axis Danse. Press kits, photograph albums, scrapbooks (1977-1985).

Les Ballets Georges Bérard, La Maison de la Danse. Souvenir program, 24 Feb. 1963.

Les Ballets Jazz. Souvenir programs and press kits (1978-1989).

Les Ballets Québec, La Maison de la Danse. Souvenir programs (1948-1949).

Marie Chouinard Collection. Press kits (1987-1989).

Gérald Crevier Collection. Souvenir programs, photographs, newspaper advertisements (1940s), press clippings (1930-1952).

Mary Cuzanne Collection. Souvenir program, New Dance Group, Montreal High School Auditorium, 26 Apr. 1938.

DansePartout. Press clippings (1980-1988).

Entre-Six. *La Séduction par la danse* (souvenir program of the 1978 season).

Juliette Fischer Collection. Scrapbooks; press clippings on Elizabeth Leese.

Lise Gagnier Collection. Photograph albums, scrapbooks; press clippings on Gérald Crevier and Georges Bérard.

Margie Gillis Collection. Souvenir programs and press kits (1978-1989).

Les Grands Ballets Canadiens, La Maison de la Danse. Souvenir programs and press kits since 1958.

Maurice Lacasse-Morenoff Collection, UQAM. Materials related to the history of the Lacasse-Morenoff school, curriculum vitae, souvenir programs (1935-1986), photograph album, scrapbooks.

Pierre Lapointe Collection, UQAM. Souvenir programs, photograph albums, press clippings (1950-1990).

Elizabeth Leese Collection, La Maison de la Danse. Scrapbooks, photographs, press clippings.

Aline Legris Collection. Photograph albums; press clippings on Gérald Crevier.

Andrée Millaire Collection. Souvenir programs, photograph albums, press clippings; scrapbooks on Ruth Sorel, Gérald Crevier, and Les Grands Ballets Canadiens.

Michael Montanaro Collection. Souvenir programs and press kits (1987-1989).

Musée d'Art Contemporain de Montréal. *Programme souvenir de la reconstruction du Récital de danse de 1948 de Françoise Sullivan et Jeanne Renaud* (April 1988).

Birouté Nagys Collection. Scrapbooks (1950-1970), photograph album, press clippings.

Pointépiénu. Press kit (1984).

Howard Richard Collection. Press kits (1987-1989).

Eddy Toussaint Collection. Souvenir programs and press kits (1980-1989).

Séda Zaré Collection, UQAM. Souvenir programs, scrapbooks, press clippings relating to her career in Europe (before 1950) and Canada (1950-1980), writings, photograph albums.

Selected Filmography and Videography

GENERAL

Ballet Festival. Produced by The National Film Board of Canada, 1949. Documentary on the 1949 Toronto Canadian Ballet Festival. Works by Les Ballets Ruth Sorel, The Winnipeg Ballet, Volkoff's Canadian Ballet, and others.

Dance for Modern Times. Produced by Mossanen Productions, 1987. Works by James Kudelka (Les Grands Ballets Canadiens), David Earle and Christopher House (Toronto Dance Theatre), Danny Grossman (Danny Grossman Dance Theatre), and Ginette Laurin (O Vertigo).

Dance from Montreal. Produced by PBS in series "Alive from Off Center." Directed by Bernard Hébért and Bruno Jobin. Works by La La La Human Steps and Montréal Danse.

La Danse. Produced by Radio-Canada, 1974. Directed by François Floquet. Interviews and works by Le Groupe de la Place Royale and Le Groupe Nouvelle Aire.

For the Love of Dance: Backstage with Seven Canadian Dance Companies. Coproduced by The National Film Board of Canada and The Canada Council, 1982. Documentary on the seven companies appearing in *Gala.*

Gala. Produced by The National Film Board of Canada, 1982. Directed by John Smith. Works by Toronto Dance Theatre, Le Groupe de la Place Royale, Les Grands Ballets Canadiens, The Royal Winnipeg Ballet, The National Ballet of Canada, Anna Wyman Dance Theatre, and Contemporary Dancers of Winnipeg.

Nouvelle Danse, Danse Actuelle. Series produced by Audio-Visual Department, UQAM, 1982. Directed by Yves Racicot and Michèle Febvre. Works by Paul-André Fortier, Martine Epoque, Iro Tembeck, and Daniel Léveillé.

Un Pas dans l'inconnu. Produced by Audio-Visual Department, UQAM, 1988. Directed by Yves Racicot and Michèle Febvre. Documentary on the signatories of *Le Refus Global.* Interviews and excerpts from works by Jeanne Renaud, Françoise Sullivan, and others.

Québec Eté Danse. Produced by JFB Films, 1983. Directed by John Brooke. Interviews and works by Paul-André Fortier, Edouard Lock, and Robert Desrosiers.

Récital de danse de Françoise Sullivan et de Jeanne Renaud. Video record of reconstruction of 1948 recital by Françoise Sullivan and Jeanne Renaud held in April 1988 at the Musée d'Art Contemporain, Montreal.

Temps Danse. Series produced by Audio-Visual Department, UQAM, 1981. Directed by Yves Racicot and Michèle Febvre. Works by Martine Epoque, Iro Tembeck, Daniel Léveillé, Paul-André Fortier, and Edouard Lock.

13 chorégraphes pour 2 danseurs. Series produced by Audio-Visual Department, UQAM, 1981. Directed by Yves Racicot and Michèle Febvre. Short works by thirteen Montreal choreographers: Françoise Sullivan, Françoise Graham, Françoise Riopelle, Martine Epoque, Iro Tembeck, Edouard Lock, Daniel Léveillé, Paul-André Fortier, Jean-Pierre Perreault, Ginette Laurin, Marie Chouinard, Monique Giard/Daniel Soulières, and Christina Coleman.

COMPANIES AND CHOREOGRAPHERS

LES BALLETS JAZZ DE MONTRÉAL:

Les Ballets-Jazz Contemporains. Produced by Radio-Québec, 1973. Directed by Pierre Gauvreau.

Les Ballets Jazz de Montréal. Produced by CBC, 1987. Directed by Pierre Morin.

THE NATIONAL BALLET OF CANADA:

Bold Steps: A Portrait of the National Ballet of Canada. Produced by Primédia Productions in collaboration with CBC, 1985. Directed by Cyril Frankel.

Flamento at 5:15. Produced by The National Film Board of Canada. Directed by Cynthia Scott.

Portrait of Celia Franca. Produced by CBC. Directed by Don Browne.

Veronica Tennant: Dancer of Distinction. Produced by CBC. Directed by Carol Moode Ede.

THE ROYAL WINNIPEG BALLET:

Arnold Spohr. Produced by Oméara Productions in collaboration with CBC, 1984. Directed by Gabriel Markiw.

Evelyn Hart's Moscow Gala. Produced by Triune Productions and Northern Cross Productions, 1987. Directed by Robert Barclay.

Fall River Legend. Produced by CBC.

Portrait of Gweneth Lloyd. Produced by CBC, 1980. Directed by Don Browne.

Romeo and Juliet. Produced by CBC. Directed by Norman Campbell.

Shadow on the Prairie. Produced by The National Film Board of Canada, 1953.

PAUL-ANDRÉ FORTIER:

Bande dansinée. In *13 chorégraphes pour 2 danseurs* (see above).

L'été latent. Produced Audio-Visual Department, UQAM, 1989. Directed by Yves Racicot.

Fin. In *Temps Danse* (see above).

Lavabos (excerpts). In *Québec Eté Danse* (see above).

Pow! t'es mort, Fin, Violence, and *Images noires*. In *Temps Danse* and *Nouvelle Danse, Danse Actuelle* (see above).

Tell. In *Dance from Montreal* (see above).

LES GRANDS BALLETS CANADIENS:

The Achievers: Ludmilla Chiriaeff. Produced by CBC, 1989.

Adieu Robert Schumann. Produced by Production Spectrum, 1980. Directed by Norman Campbell.

Ballerina. Produced by The National Film Board of Canada, 1963. Portrait of Margaret Mercier.

Ballet Adagio. Produced by The National Film Board of Canada, 1971. Directed by Norman McLaren.

Catulli Carmina. Produced by CBC, 1980. Directed by Mario Prizek.

For the Love of Dance: Backstage with Seven Canadian Dance Companies (see above).

Gala (see above).

Les Grands Ballets Canadiens at 30. Produced by CBC, 1988. Directed by Peter Au.

In Paradisum. In *Dance for Modern Times* (see above).

Le Mandarin merveilleux. Produced by Radio Canada, 1981. Directed by Pierre Morin.

Narcisse. Produced by The National Film Board of Canada, 1983. Directed by Norman McLaren.

Pas de Deux. Produced by The National Film Board of Canada, 1969. Directed by Norman McLaren.

Portrait of Ludmilla Chiriaeff. Produced by CBC, 1979. Directed by Lorraine Thompson.

Sur les scènes de l'Orient. Coproduced by The National Film Board of Canada and Radio Canada, 1985. Directed by John Smith.

Tam ti de lam. Produced by CBC, 1977. Directed by Pierre Morin.

Visage: Ludmilla Chiriaeff. Produced by Radio-Québec. Directed by Marius Téodoresco.

LE GROUPE NOUVELLE AIRE:

B...comme Bientôt (Martine Epoque). Video record. Audio-Visual Department, UQAM.

La Cellule humaine (Martine Epoque). Visual record. CEGEP Montmorency.

La Danse. Produced by Radio Canada, 1974. Directed by François Floquet. Interviews and excerpts from *Mi-é-Meta* and *Rituel*.

De Profundis (Martine Epoque). Video record. CEGEP Montmorency.

Dibs (Martine Epoque). Video record. Audio-Visual Department, UQAM.

L'envers du décor avec Le Groupe Nouvelle Aire. Produced by Radio-Québec, 1978. Directed by Raynald Letourneau. Interviews and excerpts from *La Trilogie de la Montagne*, *Remous*, and *Fil d'images*.

Evanescence (Martine Epoque). Video record. CEGEP Montmorency.

Lianes (Martine Epoque). Video record. Audio-Visual Department, UQAM.

Madame est servie (Martine Epoque). Video record. Audio-Visual Department, UQAM.

Magnificat (Martine Epoque). Video record. CEGEP Montmorency.

Ni scène ni coulisses. Produced by The National Film Board of Canada, 1978. Directed by Denis Poulin.

On n'a plus les séances qu'on avait. Produced by Radio-Québec, 1972. Directed by Pierre Gauvreau. Interviews and excerpts from *Amiboïsme* and *De Profundis*.

Point, Virgule (Martine Epoque). Video record. Audio-Visual Department, UQAM.

Rituel (Martine Epoque). Video record. CEGEP Montmorency.

Tour à tour (Martine Epoque). Video record. Audio-Visual Department, UQAM.

L'univers de Martine Epoque. Produced by Radio-Québec, 1986. Directed by Marius Téodorescu.

Vivre à deux (Martine Epoque). Video record. Audio-Visual Department, UQAM.

Yul 86 (Martine Epoque). Video record. Audio-Visual Department, UQAM.

Rehearsal videos of Nouvelle Aire's *Densité*, *Fil d'images*, *Sources*, *Images noires*, *Trilogie*, *Howl*, *Incubes*, and *Non Hal...*.

LE GROUPE DE PLACE ROYALE:

Calliope. Produced by Danse Partout, 1987. Version remounted by Jean-Pierre Perreault on Danse Partout.

La Danse (see above).

Expression 65. Video copy of 1965 silent film. UQAM Archives.

For the Love of Dance: Backstage with Seven Canadian Dance Companies (see above).

Gala (see above).

Karanas. Video copy of silent film. UQAM Archives.

MARGIE GILLIS:

Body Emotions: Margie Gillis. Produced by CBC, 1977. Directed by Bernard Picard.

L'univers de Margie Gillis. Produced by Radio-Québec, 1978.

MAURICE LACASSE-MORENOFF:

Les Démons du midi. Produced by CBC, 1987. Directed by André Forte.

GINETTE LAURIN:

Asphaltes. Rehearsal video. Audio-Visual Department, UQAM.

Chevy Dream. Filmed by Jean-Philippe Trépanier. Vancouver, 1985.

Crash Landing. Performance record. Festival International de Nouvelle Danse (FIND), 1985.

Etude II. Promotional video. Produced by Danse Partout, 1987.

Etude II. Performance record. Festival International de Nouvelle Danse (FIND), 1985.

Full House. In *Dance for Modern Times* (see above).

Olé. Performance record. Festival International de Nouvelle Danse (FIND), 1985.

L'univers de Ginette Laurin et O Vertigo. Produced by Radio-Québec, 1987.

DANIEL LÉVEILLÉ:

A force d'y penser, on y pense de moins en moins. Audio-Visual Department, UQAM, 1988.

Fleurs du peau. In *Temps Danse* and *Nouvelle Danse, Danse Actuelle* (see above).

L'Inceste. In *Temps Danse* and *Nouvelle Danse, Danse Actuelle* (see above).

Jericho. In *Dance from Montreal* (see above).

Jeu. In *Temps Danse* and *Nouvelle Danse, Danse Actuelle* (see above).

Le Sacre du Printemps. In *Temps Danse* and *Nouvelle Danse, Danse Actuelle* (see above).

Voyeurisme. In *Temps Danse* and *Nouvelle Danse, Danse Actuelle* (see above).

EDOUARD LOCK:

Human Sex. Produced by Skalgoyannis Exclusive Management, 1985.

Human Sex. Aired on CBC, 1987.

Oranges ou la recherche du Paradis (Oranges, or the Search for Paradise). In *Temps Danse* (see above).

Remous (excerpt). In *L'envers du décor avec Le Groupe Nouvelle Aire.* Produced by Radio-Québec, 1978. Directed by Raynald Letourneau.

Western. In *13 chorégraphes pour 2 danseurs* (see above).

JEAN-PIERRE PERREAULT:

Calliope. Promotional video. Produced by Danse Partout, 1987.

Dix Minutes. In *13 chorégraphes pour 2 danseurs* (see above).

Joe. Video record of dress rehearsal. Audio-Visual Department, UQAM, 1988.

Nuit. Produced by Audio-Visual Department, UQAM, 1986. Directed by Claude Beaulieu.

Stella. Performance record. Festival International de Nouvelle Danse (FIND), 1985.

LINDA RABIN:

O Parade. Produced by Audio-Visual Department, UQAM, 1980.

JEANNE RENAUD:

Deformité. In *Récital de danse de Françoise Sullivan et de Jeanne Renaud* (see above).

L'Emprise. In *Récital de danse de Françoise Sullivan et de Jeanne Renaud* (see above).

Expression 65. Video copy of 1965 silent film. UQAM Archives.

Karanas. Video copy of silent film. UQAM Archives.

Moi je suis de cette race rouge (with Françoise Sullivan). In *Récital de danse de Françoise Sullivan et de Jeanne Renaud* (see above).

Un Pas dans l'inconnu (see above).

HOWARD RICHARD:

A Woman, A Man, and a Woman. Video record. Artscène, UQAM, 1989.

Les Baigneurs. Video record. Artscène, UQAM, 1989.

Colors. Video record. Artscène, UQAM, 1989.

Cross Currents. Video record. Artscène, UQAM, 1989.

Woman Reclining on a Chair. Video record. Artscène, UQAM, 1989.

FRANÇOISE RIOPELLE:

Tout autour et dans le fond. In *13 chorégraphes pour 2 danseurs* (see above).

HUGO ROMERO:

L'Oiseau de feu. Produced by Radio-Canada, 1982. Directed by Pierre Morin.

FRANÇOISE SULLIVAN:

A tout prendre. In *13 chorégraphes pour 2 danseurs* (see above).

Black and Tan. In *Récital de danse de Françoise Sullivan et de Jeanne Renaud* (see above).

Dédale. In *Récital de danse de Françoise Sullivan et de Jeanne Renaud* (see above).

Dualité. In *Récital de danse de Françoise Sullivan et de Jeanne Renaud* (see above).

La Femme archaïque. In *Récital de danse de Françoise Sullivan et de Jeanne Renaud* (see above).

Gothique. In *Récital de danse de Françoise Sullivan et de Jeanne Renaud* (see above).

Moi je suis de cette race rouge (with Jeanne Renaud). In *Récital de danse de Françoise Sullivan et de Jeanne Renaud* (see above).

Et la Nuit à la Nuit. Produced by Audio-Visual Department, UQAM, 1981. Directed by Yves Racicot.

EDDY TOUSSAINT:

Cantates (excerpts). Promotional video. Production Martine Blais, 1989.

Façades (excerpts). Promotional video. Production Martine Blais, 1989.

Missa Criolla. Produced by Radio-Canada. Directed by Pierre Morin.

Un Simple Moment. Produced by Radio-Canada. Directed by Pierre Morin.

Souvenances (excerpts). Promotional video. Production Martine Blais, 1989.

Symphonie du Nouveau Monde (New World Symphony) (excerpts). Promotional video. Production Martine Blais, 1989.

Variation sur un air connu (excerpts). Promotional video. Production Martine Blais, 1989.

SÉDA ZARÉ:

Anatomie pratique. Floor barre demonstration. Filmed by CEGEP Montmorency, 1972.

Index

Note: Numbers in *italics* refer to illustrations.